PROVOCATIONS

THE WAR ON THE OLD

JOHN SUTHERLAND

SERIES EDITOR:

YASMIN ALIBHAI-BROWN

\B^b\
Biteback Publishing

First published in Great Britain in 2016 by
Biteback Publishing Ltd
Westminster Tower
3 Albert Embankment
London SE1 7SP
Copyright © John Sutherland 2016

ISBN 978-1-78590-171-3

10 9 8 7 6 5 4 3 2 1

A CIP catalogue record for this book is available from the British Library.

Set in Stempel Garamond

Printed and bound in Great Britain by
CPI Group (UK) Ltd, Croydon CR0 4YY

MIX
Paper from
responsible sources
FSC® C020471
www.fsc.org

Youth is wasted on the Young.

– GEORGE BERNARD SHAW (DIED AGED 94)

We're all living longer –
which is a good thing, of course.

– EVERY LYING POLITICIAN COURTING THE GREY VOTE

Perhaps the War to come will not be between the rich
and the poor, but between the Young and the Old.

– NIALL FERGUSON

(AGE 52 – AND WHICH SIDE WILL HE FIGHT ON?)

Who wants to be called 'mature', like an old cheese?
We all know that 'mature' means on the verge of
incontinence, idiocy and peevish valetudinarianism.

– JEREMY PAXMAN (AGE 66, RETORTING TO THE MAGAZINE
MATURE TIMES, WHICH DARED PRINT A PIECE ABOUT HIM)

Contents

Preface

THIS, AS THE title of the series ('Provocations') proclaims, is a polemic. At times, perhaps, a rant. In it I iterate and reiterate a main point: that there is a covert, but state-condoned, campaign against the nation's old. By analogy with 'ethnic cleansing' it could be called 'demographic cleansing'. I have called it 'war'. Call it what you will, it's happening; there are casualties – hundreds of thousands of them – and it's wrong. Very wrong.

Where the treatment of the British elderly is concerned, we would really rather not know. Even when the facts are staring us in the eye. I open *The Times* of 16 August 2016, for example (it is today's issue as I'm writing). The first five pages of the paper are taken up by hosannas for apple-cheeked young Britons winning 'gold' for their country in far-off Rio. Hip hip.

On page 11 of the paper, my eye is struck by three, ostensibly unthrilling, stories. The main article on the page is entitled 'Dementia Patients Face a Care Lottery'. It opens: 'Dementia patients are facing a post-code lottery with figures showing that the quality of care varies wildly around the country … in some areas, patients routinely go a year without having their condition reviewed.'

For 'reviewed', read 'given a damn about'. The article – unexcitedly written (the news is, after all, wholly unexciting) – notes that 'more than 850,000 people in Britain have dementia'. A goodly number, one would have thought. Twice the circulation of the newspaper. Four times the size of the current UK army. For most of those sufferers the chances of getting adequate care are less than hopeful. If they do, as in every 'lottery', it is down to luck.

Below the fold, on the same page 11 of *The Times*, there is a story entitled 'Thousands Have Surgery Cancelled at Last Minute'. Again, the figures are considerable. The piece reports: 'Nearly 77,000 patients had operations cancelled on the day that they had been due to take place last year. Each day, 210 operations for hip replacements, cataracts and other non-urgent surgeries were called off at the last minute.'

The specified ailments are, of course, those most common, universal almost, among the aged. They might regard (readily curable) physical immobility and (readily curable) blindness as rather urgent surgery. But who, among the younger tens of millions, cares about those old wrecks? Take a ticket and go to the end of the queue, old-timers; there's a child with a broken ankle who needs 'urgent' attention.

A third story on the same page 11, snuggled into the right-hand corner, is headlined 'Abrupt Receptionists Deter the Sick from Visiting GPs'. Deterrence takes the form of rude, barking, dismissive voices at the other end of the phone – receptionists doing as they are encouraged to do by the GPs themselves.

The article explains: 'Academics have confirmed that many patients are having to struggle with unhelpful receptionists to get seen by the NHS.' But who is most susceptible to this widespread bugger-off in the surgery? The old, frail, timid and servile. People in my state of life, if I'm honest.

All this is in a newspaper but it's not news. Call it confirmation, were any needed, of 'normalised neglect' – something so 'institutional' that it barely merits passing mention on page 11 of the nation's newspaper of record. Indeed, one suspects, the neglect is bigger than merely institutional: it's nationally condoned. Climatic, insofar as the state can make the weather for us. But don't make a noise about it. There's that interesting story about that adorable young Lott couple: love and jockstraps.

The *Telegraph* – we're still with 16 August 2016, incidentally – has the following story that day. The paper caters for a 'mature' readership and the report is given some prominence:

> Elderly people needing to go into a care home now face average fees of £30,000 a year, as costs are rising ten times faster than pensioner incomes, a study has found.
>
> A study by Prestige nursing, one of the UK's biggest

care agencies, has shed light on the UK's 'desperate and worsening' care crisis, with the annual cost of a care home room increasing by £1,536, or 5.2pc over the past year. This is almost ten times more than the average £156 (1pc) income gains earned by pensioners over the same period, suggesting that paying for care without spending savings is becoming unaffordable even for the wealthiest pensioners.

The paper quoted Ros Altmann, the former pensions minister, as saying:

> Anyone who has some savings will have to spend all their money on care before receiving means tested council support and those who need to go into residential care face crippling costs as fees keep rising. Most people will be forced to sell their homes unless they can find money elsewhere.

Where, one may ask, does that money, if they 'find' it, go? Obviously a chunk goes into the 'care' which is glossily advertised in the 'homes' brochures. But another sizeable chunk dribbles into the pockets of the privatised profiteers running the system. You didn't, did you, think it was a 'charity'? You don't have the money? Sod off. We don't care.

Those wanting material more blood-curdling than hundreds of thousands of oldsters contemplating their country's indifference to their plight may usefully have called up Google News the same day (16 August) and slotted in 'Elderly Abuse' on the search bar.

The grisly chronicle of Ashbourne House care home is promptly shot onto the screen. The establishment, located in Middleton, Greater Manchester and run, with a clutch of other so-called 'homes', by the commercial firm Silverdale, 'provides accommodation for up to 29 people over 65 who require nursing or personal care – including residents with dementia and learning disabilities'. Silverdale is a comforting name – calling up imagery of silver strands among the gold and the rolling countryside of Lancashire. 'Our Company's Core Values' are proudly proclaimed online:

Silverdale Care Homes Ltd has established a 'Philosophy

Of Care' approach which is reflected in its high standards of care and promotion of residents' independence. Our philospohy [*sic*] translates into practice – and our residents receive the best of care through our person-centered approach that respects privacy and maintains dignity.

On 16 August, as the ever-ready Mr Google reminds us, two Ashbourne nurses ('carers') have been convicted and are awaiting sentence for the unusual version of 'person-centred' care they practised while in Silverdale employ. The story first came to light on 25 January 2016. The *Daily Mail* made it a front-page story under the headline 'Shocking video captures two care home workers taunting dementia sufferers by torturing the "comfort dolls" they believe are real babies'.

Such dolls are given to women with dementia to soothe them. 'Some vulnerable residents', the *Mail* added, poignantly, 'come to see the toys as their own real children.'

Imaginative therapy, one would have thought. But a secret camera had been installed at Ashbourne. It showed nurses 'taunting residents by torturing their dolls'. As the paper reported – with lavish clinching illustration:

> Sickening video footage shot at Ashbourne House nursing home ... appears to show a member of staff throwing the doll to the floor, distressing its elderly owner. And photographs show the dolls being hanged, put in a tumble dryer and apparently being cooked in a saucepan on a hob ... Another photograph shows an elderly woman appearing distressed as her doll is snatched out of her hands, while there are also images of a doll face down in a fish tank...
>
> A source claims that one picture, showing the doll hung with rope around the neck outside a resident's bedroom window, was taken as the pensioner was sleeping after staff barged in and put the light on. It is thought that the pictures and video were taken and shared among some members of staff via WhatsApp ... The video, apparently filmed in a corridor of the home, shows one member of staff hurling a baby doll at the floor, shouting 'die baby, die!'. Her colleague, who is filming the shocking scene, asks: 'How do you feel that you've just done that? How

do you feel?' The woman laughs loudly in response, saying: 'Great, because [resident's name] is upset.'

Two members of staff were 'suspended' after the article (suspended by the neck, over a pot of boiling water,
relatives of the patients may have fantasised). An 'investigation' was launched, criminal proceedings followed
and a judgment was passed on 16 August. The defence
that it was merely 'silly pranks' did not hold up in court.
And, of course, had there been no clandestine cameras
there would have been no consequences for the jolly
pranksters.

What had these poor old ladies done wrong to deserve
such torment and fundamental insult to their humanity?
Nothing. They'd merely hung around planet earth too
long, outliving their usefulness or their ability to fight
back. Most, one suspects, had outlived their husbands.

What the Ashbourne customers (don't call them
patients) were put through was manifestly criminal.
But it is the attitude underlying the cruel criminality
that chills. These poor old ladies, paying between £400
and £800 a week, simply did not matter in the eyes of

those paid to look after them. They were good for a laugh: that's all.

Why do I care enough about such things to go to the trouble of writing a book? The question is easily answered. I too have hung around too long – 78 and rising at the time of writing. I do not feel *for* those old people at Ashbourne bloody care home (the place is still in business as I write, by the way), I feel *with* them. Ask not for whom the Dementia Doll Pot boils: it boils for thee, Sutherland.

I still, I think, have my wits about me. With luck I'll go to the grave that way. And what will carry me off, I wonder? If you want a good hint as to how you'll die, look at your parents' and grandparents' death certificates. My family weaknesses are lungs and alcoholism. I've had trouble with both.[1]

Despite this legacy I have lived longer than any of my ancestors I'm aware of or whose genealogical records

---

1 My wrestle with the demon drink is chronicled in my drunkalog *Last Drink to LA* (2001, repr. 2015). I developed late-life bronchial asthma at the same age as my mother, in my early seventies. It killed her, complicated as it was by a lifetime's smoking and emphysema. I've never smoked, medicines are better now, and I live on.

I've come across. And I have had, it would seem, a luckier, if not necessarily happier, life than my progenitors did. I was released from the working class into which I was born by the 1944 Butler Education Act and, after National Service (hugely enjoyable), drifted into academic life (even more enjoyable). I've never drifted out. I have had the privilege of cohabiting professionally with fine minds – colleagues cleverer than me and great literature.

I shall carry to my grave (unless I commit some act of spectacular moral turpitude – more difficult as you get older) the comical title Lord Northcliffe Professor Emeritus, UCL. 'Emeritus' means scrapheap.

It's like walking with a tombstone strapped to your back. But life, so far, has been good to me. May it spare me, and you, dear reader, the terminal horrors of the Ashbourne care home.

Part

Part I

Declining to Die

Superfluous lags the veteran on the stage.

— SAMUEL JOHNSON (DIED AGED 75)

IN JANUARY 2012, the Office for National Statistics announced some good news – a commodity in short supply during that bleak midwinter. Most statistics the papers came out with merely added to the seasonal shivers. Not least the grim fact that the price of household fuel had shot up 15 per cent as the mercury plunged down into an unusually bitter holiday season. Where was Wenceslas (age unknown, but well into the vale of years) when you needed him?

Mortality rates for men, the 'rapidly ageing'[2] nation was

---

2   This fatuous comment has become irritatingly common – particularly to pedants like myself. Of course all people age at the same rate.

informed, had fallen by almost 50 per cent since the 1970s and those for women had fallen by a third. As the *Telegraph* (21 January 2012) headlined it: 'Death Rate in Britain at Lowest Level as Most Live into 80s'. The drop (i.e. rise) was ascribed to better medical care and healthier lifestyles, which had spectacularly reduced death from heart disease.

Perhaps the winter fuel allowance helped.

Catastrophic heart attack is a mercifully quick way out. Like pneumonia, similarly reduced in modern times from its former lethality, it is nicknamed 'the old man's friend' because it allows a relatively painless goodbye from the world.[3] Just one massive kick in the chest, a second or two for the question 'What the fuck?!', and it's all over. Hello darkness, my old friend.

It's not merely that we're, as a nation,[4] living a lot – an awful lot – longer. Death, as Ecclesiastes reminds us, as the dirt rattles on the coffin, will always have its victory and the grave its sting. But we're dying more gradually. And we live more gradually. We 'take our time', as the saying goes.

---

3 'Old person's friend' somehow doesn't have the same punch.

4 As a species, the seven billion and rising of us are not all doing that well as regards longevity. In the third world, lifespans are short.

4

Think on this. Shakespeare died aged 52. And he had lifetime enough for six years' full retirement as Stratford's most revered resident. He wrote all those wonderful plays and poems ten years short of his bus-pass year and ten years short of the age of the average *Daily Telegraph* reader (before the paper's head of books, Gaby Wood, age 45, puts my name on the 'Do Not Resuscitate' list of reviewers, as, alas, I am on three major opinion-forming journals, I have confessed to being 78 and rising. Hopefully). The current proportion of the UK population aged 65+ was, in the early years of the new century, around 12 per cent. Before the 2020s, on current rates, it will be 20 per cent, as the Office for National Statistics confirmed in August 2016. There are eight million plus over-70s in the UK. More attain that age every year than come (unwelcomed) into the country as immigrants. Put another way, the UK is migrating, internally, into mass senescence. This imbalance of old over young has never happened before in Britain. Something must be done! But what?

The statistics have become drearily familiar. In the 1960s, there were eight workers for every retired 'unworker' or youthful 'pre-worker'. In the third millennium, the ratio is shrinking to three to one.

Workers' knees buckled at the very thought of it. Older brows furrowed. Politicians dithered and changed the subject. In the fourth estate, Kim Kardashian's bottom and Wayne Rooney's hair transplant made more enticing headlines than whatever 'plight' was afflicting the aged, and the country obliged to put up with the growing army of old codgers. Or put them somewhere they wouldn't be noticed. And hopefully move them without too much delay to their last resting place.

War? Surely You Exaggerate, Professor (Emeritus) Sutherland?[5]

I can imagine a sort of civil war between the old and the young in ten or fifteen years' time.

— MARTIN AMIS (AGE 67)

---

5   I have been retired (forcibly) for twelve years. Mandatory age retirement was abolished, by EU human rights legislation, shortly after I was pushed out.

Even for a series called 'Provocations', the term 'war' may seem a tad too provocative – or lazy. We (over) use the term hyperbolically and metaphorically; as in, for example, 'war on drugs', or 'war on want' (what on earth does that mean?).[6]

Those of my vintage can remember a 'real war'. It was a 'declared' thing, out in the open. Ultimata were fiercely delivered to embassies, armies recruited and conscripted, civilian populations 'mobilised' for the 'war effort'. Blood, in continental quantities, was spilled. Things were done behind barbed wire, and in the open, too horrible to contemplate.

My father (dead aged 31) was killed, burned to death, in an RAF plane, in a foreign place I have never visited. Our house was bombed by aircraft from the other side. I recall my mother scooping me up to carry me, incendiaries burning like *Walpurgisnacht*, to the nearest shelter. It was in what had once been dungeons in Colchester Castle, a building which had seen many wars since Boudicca and the Romans.

---

6   There's a good Wikipedia entry on the misuse of the 'war on [whatever]' formula: https://en.wikipedia.org/wiki/War_as_metaphor.

I can smell the dungeon damp still. My eye was caught by a red-painted bucket of sand in a corner. I can see it now more clearly than I can see the screen in front of me.

Nonetheless, extravagant as it may be, I think the phrase 'war on the old' is justifiable in current circumstances, although it is a war without bombs, bullets or red buckets full of sand.

War takes different forms in the modern world. It is asymmetric, non-conflictual, fluid, and longer-lasting than the precise four and six years of the two so-called world wars. At its least combative fringe, the war against the old I'm talking about is non-violent opposition with attitude – the snarl, the snide, barely heard, comment, even 'the funny look'.

Like others of my age with whom I've discussed it, I've noticed that – walking a busy street – I'm invisible. People bump into me, as if I weren't there. I reel; they don't even look behind or register my protesting mumble.

I worked out why it was. The women have no interest in me: I'm not a potential mate (indeed I'm not) or sugar daddy ('What first attracted you to the millionaire

8

Professor Sutherland, Ms Golddigger?'). My sexuality quotient is less than zero. I avoid mirrors nowadays.

And the men, ever ready for combat, see me as no threat. A masculine zilch. And so I bump along the sidewalk, getting bumped on the way. I'm there and not there. This is how it must feel to be a ghost.

The attitude goes along with sharper, more lethal fronts. And casualties. Horribly many of them. Old people are being neglected or institutionally abused, even dying, in large numbers – unnecessarily and wrongly.

They are victims not of old-style bayonet-in-the-guts or bomb-from-the-sky warfare but of programmatic negligence – negligence so widespread that, common sense suggests, there must surely be a policy behind it. A canny affirmative wink.

Someone, somewhere, means it.

One of the questions posed by this 'provocative' book is whether 'willed' indifference and neglect, on a totalitarian scale, with cruel consequences, are witness to a new kind of intra-social warfare or whether it is just what has always gone on, inter-generationally, raised to a higher pitch than normal.

Gerontophobia can certainly be seen to bubble up as a perennial fact of human societies. It's part of the package.[7] In *Oedipus Rex*, the young hero has a road-rage moment with an annoying old codger at a crossroads. What does he do? He kills him. Why? Because he's in the way. And, although he only dimly knows it, he wants what the old guy (his father, did he but know it) has: the kingship of Thebes and the old guy's young wife (his mother, did Oedipus but know it). The trappings. They should be his. He's young, for God's sake (Sophocles' gods do not agree – as King Oedipus will find out). The Oedipus complex, Freud instructed us, is universal. Part of its deal is: 'kill the old'. Or, at least, fantasise about it.

There are, even in this straightforward Sophoclean example, some interesting complexities which will strike the reflective person. Laius and Oedipus are successive monarchs of Thebes. In Sophocles' play, Oedipus is himself old(ish) – he has grown-up children. He is normally played on stage around King Lear's age.

---

7   Being a professor, I have laced my argument with literary examples. Literature everywhere in the area I know best (literature in English) bears out the 'perennial intergenerational friction' thesis.

The UK currently has a monarch who has ruled for sixty-four years and lived for ninety ('long live our gracious queen', as the national anthem puts it – Elizabeth II has fulfilled that part of her sovereign responsibility better than any of her predecessors). Her Majesty's heir apparent (age 68) qualified for his bus pass and winter fuel allowance eight years ago.

We have, as I write, a PM, Theresa May (age 60), who – if she lasts that long (and her regime refrains from abolishing the goody) – will qualify for her bus pass in six years' time. The most powerful press mogul in the Western world, Rupert Murdoch, is 85 years old. He gives no sign of wanting to abdicate (or ride buses, come to that). Leadership of the world's most powerful nation will be contested, as this book goes to press, between a man aged 70 and a woman aged 69. The *Sunday Times* and *Forbes* lists of the richest human beings are dominated by senior citizens (predominantly male). There are also, if one extends the gaze, 'national treasures', culture heroes who are well on in life: Alan Bennett, Mary Berry, Vivienne Westwood, Judi Dench, David Hockney.

These stars and potentates, however, represent nothing, demographically. They are figureheads: as much exceptions to the rule as the very young super-rich, like Mark Zuckerberg (age 32). Or super-athletes, like the current crop of British gold medallists as I write, who by no means reflect the state of the nation's physical health and prowess (given the arguments raging about the 'sugar tax', Billy Bunter would be the more appropriate emblem for the obese Britons, and their youthful offspring, *de nos jours*).

The intractable point remains. The 'old' – en masse, in their insect millions – are a 'problem'. Worse than that, for the junior masses ranked against them, they have become, very recently, 'a hostile entity' to be 'dealt with'. Neutered politically, eased into invisible, but remorseless, non-existence. Or hurried on, out of the way, to make room.

Not, of course, that any such a policy could ever be declared – Neville Chamberlain (died aged 71) style, waving a piece of paper. But yes, it's a war.

The Casus Belli

I hope I die before I get old.

– PETE TOWNSHEND, 1965. MR TOWNSHEND IS CURRENTLY 71

YEARS OLD. REALLY OLD.

In general, the young are not predisposed to like the old and never have been. The old are living reminders of what awaits. What the old represent, in terms of lifespan, fascinates and appals those not yet there but unstoppably on the way – if they're 'lucky' (a word loaded with irony).

Among the more visited giveaway ('sponsored') sites on news websites are picture galleries under titles such as 'Which famous star has aged worst?', 'What the cast of [fill in a title] look like now: you won't recognise them'. The sites are brutally iconoclastic. The once beautiful are shown in a condition of their current wormy decay. Millions of hits are drawn to such sites, which are laden with expensive advertising.[8]

---

8   Try http://foreverceleb.com/20-celebrities-that-aged-terribly.

The Apollos and Aphrodites were once lovely and handsome, but are enviable no more. Ho bloody ho! The images provoke mixed, unworthy feelings in the voyeur. 'How the mighty are fallen' is one, when we see the wreckage that used to be Mickey Rourke's or Meg Ryan's physiognomy.

But, at the same time, the youthful and middle-aged do not wish to be reminded of what is coming for them – as it came to those once beautiful ones. Nip and tuck and plaster as you will, but (to paraphrase Hamlet) to this end must thou come is what those websites say to us. Each young person has a Dorian Gray self-portrait hidden in their attic. Themselves, aged 60+. They yearn to destroy it.

Open War

An aged man is but a paltry thing,
A tattered coat upon a stick, unless
Soul clap its hands and sing, and louder sing

– W. B. YEATS (DIED AGED 73), 'SAILING TO BYZANTIUM'

What could be called an ever-rumbling subterranean friction between the generations erupted into open intergenerational war on an unexpected front on the night of 23 June 2016.

There were two causes. That of longer standing was the Baby Boomer Bulge, seven decades on. Soldiers had come marching home from WWII, gonads fairly busting with the desire to be fruitful and multiply.[9] What was the command Shaka gave to his victorious Zulu impis after victory? 'Now wipe the blade!' I remember finding condoms in the street on the morning walk to school (three miles). Those that had not been used (surprisingly many – I lived in a garrison town) I sold to schoolmates as balloons.

Over those eighteen post-war months, which also swept Churchill out of power, the nation swam in an ocean of sperm and unprecedented insemination. The grammar school I was at, in 1959, had to add a whole new stream to make room for the 30 per cent post-war 'Bulge', as it was called.

---

9   Had my father not been killed in the early years of the war, I would, for a
    certainty, have had siblings. I was, frankly, glad not to.

It was as if, for eighteen glorious months, the whole country was busting out all over with a glorious future in prospect. The BBB generation duly came of age in the late 1960s and early 1970s, breaking old moulds and patterns of life all the way. They were – there is no other word for it – 'life force'. Gale force eleven.

Society trembled and shook spasmodically as the Bulge passed through the decades.

Abortion? Legalise it.

Homosexuality? Decriminalise it.

Pornography? Let Lady Chat open the way into decensorship, and fuck Mrs Whitehouse.

Feminism? Scrap the feminine mystique and female eunuch.

Police? Pigs.

Drugs? They're OK. In fact, better than OK. They're needful.

Capital punishment? Abolish it, except for bureaucrats.

Europe? Join it.

Hair? Grow it and show it.

Pregnancy? Take a pill and forget it.

STD? Take another pill and forget that as well. While you're at it, try a purple heart.

Higher education? It's a right, not a privilege – don't be grateful. Rebel, put on a Mao hat and oppose book worship.

The world? See it – ideally, hitch to Nepal to see it.

Sex? Never stop (menopause bothering you? Try HRT. Erectile function bothering you? Pop some Viagra).

As a spectator (I am marginally pre-BBB), it was exhilarating to witness the creative destruction wrought by this cohort, rearranging British society like Lego as they went forward from childhood to youth to adulthood to middle age, carrying with them pension benefits and fine housing that neither their predecessors nor their successors could enjoy, or hope to enjoy. They plundered.

In 2016, the Baby Boomer Bulge, now 70, crashed, like a tsunami, into retirement. Traditionally, the old had turned up their toes, faced the wall and exited without fuss. As Terry Eagleton (Marxist sage of the BBB, age

73) put it, the gravestones of his parents' generation should have been inscribed with 'We gave no trouble'.[10]

Not so the baby boomers. Trouble was their middle name. In elections they voted en masse, strategically and astutely – principally on single issues important to their cohort. Notice was taken by whatever government of the day. Plans to abolish the triple-lock initiative (which protects the old-age pension) were nixed, for example, in July 2016, when advisers told the new PM that it would piss off the grey vote mightily. And without that vote, Mrs May, hello back benches.

A self-assertive army of retirees (don't call them wrinklies: botox handled that little problem) were changing the sunset years of the UK population. In image and fact. How was it Shakespeare described the seventh age of man? 'Sans teeth, sans eyes, sans taste, sans everything.' The BBBs entered that decade with proud erections and piranha gleaming teeth. They did not give up their

---

10 Eagleton makes the point in his memoir, *The Gatekeeper* (2002). Like many of his generation, myself included, Eagleton's attitude to his servile parents' generation is a mixture of scorn and love.

'everything' readily. Their portraits in the attic looked a lot better than those of their ancestors.

A popular American bumper sticker summed up the BBB mood: 'I'm spending my children's patrimony': typically they surge past in an enviably good vehicle.

Spending the kids' money was, unsurprisingly, resented by those denied it. 'Two Brains' David Willetts (age 60) – the cleverest Tory – called them the 'Pinch Generation'. 'So bloody what?' was the BBBs' shout back.

> *I can't speak to my dad.*
>
> – *GUARDIAN* HEADLINE IN THE AFTERMATH
>
> OF THE EU REFERENDUM

The triggering moment was around two o'clock in the morning, 24 June 2016. I had gone to bed around 11 p.m. that night, secure in the pollsters' forecast and William Hill's odds. 'Remain' would coast to victory. Yawn. Happy dreams. All's well with the world.

It wasn't. My wife burst into the bedroom at 3 o/c with the screech: 'Wake up, I can't face this alone. The fools are voting for Brexit.' What fools? The snap judgement the next day was: the old fools. Who could doubt it? In *The Times*, on Saturday 25 June, Giles Coren (then aged 46) delivered himself of a scathing *j'accuse*. The article was entitled and subtitled 'Wrinklies have well and truly stitched us up: The referendum shows that old folk can't be trusted with big decisions. They're always wrong. About everything.'

That pretty well indicated who the *accusés* were.

'The wrinkly bastards', continued Coren, 'stitched us young 'uns [46!] up good and proper on Thursday':

> For make no mistake, it is the old people who did this to us. I assume you have seen the voting breakdown by age? In the 18–24 group it was 64 per cent to Remain and 24 per cent to Leave. In the 25–49 age group it was 45 per cent to 39. Only in the 50–64 bracket does the balance shift, going over to 49 per cent for Leave, as against 35 for Remain. And then among the over-65s it was an astonishing 58 per cent for Leave, against 33 per cent for Remain.

The article then exploded into a shit-storm of unbridled ageist tirade: 'From their stairlifts and their Zimmer frames, their electric recliner beds and their walk-in baths, they reached out with their wizened old writing hands to make their wobbly crosses and screwed their children and their children's children for a thousand generations.'

One recalls Charlton Heston (died aged 85) at the end of *Planet of the Apes*: 'You maniacs! You blew it up! Ah, damn you! God damn you all to hell!' Young Coren confessed to his readers: 'I formed my eventual decision to vote Remain. I just knew that I could not vote with the old people. Because old people are always wrong. About everything.'

Coren's conclusion was, with menace, the necessary disenfranchisement of the aged – by which he meant anyone over the age of 60:

> And don't go telling me that we owe at least a debt of respect to the elderly. Respect for what? Don't confuse the elderly of today with the elderly of the recent past. This lot did not fight a war (not many of them). They didn't free us from the yoke of tyranny. They didn't live in modesty and hardship and hunger so that

future generations might thrive. They just enjoyed high employment, good pay, fat benefits, enormous pension privileges, international travel, the birth of pop music and lashings of free sex. We don't owe them a thing. We should cut them off. Rewrite the franchise to start at 16 and end at 60 and do this thing all over again.

We won't, of course. So we will be compelled to make our strength of feeling felt in smaller, subtler ways. In fact it is already happening. As early as lunchtime on Friday, Twitter was showing 15,000 retweets of what may come to be the standout mantra for Brexit 2016: 'I'm never giving up my seat on the train for an old person again.'

One recalls Bertolt Brecht's joke. If the people vote the wrong way, elect a new people. But for a newspaper whose constituency is substantially elderly, and whose proprietor – Coren's paymaster – is not in the first flush of youth, this was fighting talk and thin ice.

The paper's 'feedback' editor, Rose Wild (age unknown, but not, judging by her byline photo, a 'young 'un'), put together an emollient explanation cum apology the following Saturday. It opened: 'Not for the first time in his life, Giles Coren has poked a sharp stick into the hornet's nest.'

Wild went on to quote some friendly responses. There were not, one apprehended, an overwhelming number for her to draw on. But she concluded with a tweeted response from Coren himself. This is how it went:

Dear Older Person

My intention in the article was to respond to some random polling breakdowns by satirizing the bigoted language of both of the referendum campaigns.

I had assumed my position was SO F***ING LUDICROUS that you could not take it seriously. It seems that in this, as in so many things in the last few days, I was wildly mistaken

Xxx Giles.

To which this 'wrinkly' is inclined to reply, 'BOLL***S, younger person.' There is no irony marker (e.g. 'just joking, folks') in the piece to undercut its eloquent ageist insults. Coren was simply letting fly.

Coren was, as was clear, just one *enragé* kicking up

his leg in a chorus line of *soi-disant* 'young 'uns'. *The Guardian* (normally admirably vigilant about any ageist *lapsus linguae*) devoted its G2 lead story on 28 June to a lament by Rhiannon Lucy Cosslett (aged 28) entitled 'I Am Ashamed of My Own Mother … How Could Dad Do This?' Her juvenile wail opened: '"I'm worried Brexit has made me ageist," a friend said, following the shock of the referendum result on Friday morning. "I saw this Jewish couple in the street and just felt this sudden, enormous wave of fury towards them and their generation. It was almost physical."'

There was a mountain of similar ageist abuse and barely controlled verbal violence on Twitter, Facebook and bloggery.

I've changed 'older' to 'Jewish' in the above quote, by the way. I could have made the point with 'wheelchaired', 'Afro-Caribbean', 'Inuit', or whatever other group we quite rightly protect from abusive language nowadays. But no verbal protection, it seems, for the elderly. Fair game.

And what, precisely, had we oldsters done to incur this falsetto wrath? Exercised our democratic rights. I, to repeat the point, voted 'Remain'; I didn't want to be bombed by those bloody Germans again. Coren's suggestion that the right to vote be withdrawn from the older generation was tantamount to electoral castration.

Numbers

Coren's clinching statistics were a trifle shaky, it later emerged. That as many as 90 per cent of the over-60s went for 'Leave' indeed seemed true(ish). Also true was his contention that it was this block vote that moved the result to its razor-blade-narrow Brexit victory.

Immediate surveys suggested, however, that only 35 per cent or so of the young had voted. The majority could, it was assumed, simply not be bothered. They should have put a 'like / don't like' tab on Facebook, one wag (someone of age, one assumed) quipped. But still later analysis of the data suggested that a higher number of youngsters (overwhelmingly 'Remain' supporters) did indeed vote – 64 per cent was the amended figure. But – and it gets complicated at this point – that was the percentage among those who were actually registered to vote. They were estimated to be a paltry 50 per cent of the youthful population.

There are good demographic reasons for the younger person finding registration difficult. They are an inherently 'floating' population. It's peculiarly difficult, if you're in your teens or early twenties, to maintain a fixed address, place of work or place of study.[11]

What seemed generally true, however, was that the old voted one way, the young the other way. And, given the closeness of the result, the 'wizened hand', as Coren called it, probably pushed the nation towards 'Leave'.

As part of that cohort, but out of step with it, I'm not sure why my contemporaries did go so overwhelmingly for Brexit. Fear of immigrants? Anger at rule by bureaucratic Brussels, whose bureaucrats, irritatingly, spoke better English than one did oneself? Nostalgia for a lost England which probably never existed? (Scotland, incidentally, voted solidly Remain – for reasons

---

11 The government had earlier stopped universities being allowed to register their students en masse and made it the responsibility of the individual student, shortly before the last general election. This meant that a lower proportion of students were registered to vote anywhere. This could be assumed to have had significant repercussions in the referendum.

very Scottish.) The historians will tell us in the fullness of time. Probably after I'm gone.

But, once a war starts, the reason for its starting is soon forgotten. Did any Allied soldier think, on D-Day, 'This, my Nazi friends, is payback for the invasion of Poland'? No. Allied blood would be shed on behalf of the 'free world'. Down with bad people like them. Up with good people like us.

It was a smokescreen, of course. The central aim in the war against the old is the same as that in all war, at its very highest levels – including, I believe, WWII, which marred my childhood. That aim? Destroy or displace the enemy physically and take over their resources, property and power.

That, in my view, is either happening or on the brink of happening in the intergenerational conflict between young and old, post-June 2016, that Britain is currently living through.

The casus belli was rendered all the sharper a month later, when, on 19 July, a report was published by the Institute for Fiscal Studies (IFS). It disclosed that 'pensioners have incomes that have "grown so much" that they are now the least likely group to be in poverty'. The most likely to be impoverished were, the IFS went on, 'those between 22 and 30 years of age'.

Commenting on the findings, Angus Hanton (a handsome-looking baby boomer with teenage children, his publicity reveals, age unknown), co-founder at the charity Intergenerational Foundation (a rabidly youthist lobby group), was reported as saying: 'This new report from the IFS provides the latest evidence that a generation of hard-working young people is being left behind by an economy which is failing to provide them with the kind of secure, fairly rewarded work which previous generations have taken for granted.'

Who was to blame? The grey-haired plutocracy. My folk.

Part II

I Must Be Cruel,
Only to Be Kind

B OIL OUT ALL the argy-bargy and it comes down, as I say, to 'spoils' and things there are not enough of – as in all wars. The old are excoriated as **bed-blockers** (denying their juniors the care they require in hospital); **house-hoarders** (denying their juniors the roof over their heads they deserve); and, closely related to the house-owning and gold-plated pensioning, **wealth-accumulators** (the luckier among them). It irks the deprived young.

It's worth taking a moment or two to review these specific grievances.

Bed-Blocking

Who's been sleeping in my bed?

Hospitals were, in my young days, places you passed through at some speed – leaving headfirst, if you survived; feet first, a sheet over your face, if you didn't. No lingering. But nowadays, vexatiously, the old do not expire from whatever ailment brought them to their hospital bed. 'Life-support' systems have become perversely sophisticated. Too often the old patient is suspended, in extended sickness and disability, between life and death. Hospitals are not set up for that assistance.

Many of the aged millions who live alone have no resident 'carer': no one, that is, on whom to deposit a sick, high-maintenance old person requiring assistance 24/7. One recalls from one's childhood bedtime stories Sinbad and the Old Man of the Sea. The intrepid young voyager finds himself wrecked in the garden of paradise. What luck! He meets a poor, decrepit old man, who asks Sinbad to carry him a little way on his shoulders. Sinbad good-naturedly obliges. A big mistake. The old man's legs lock like a vice around Sinbad's neck and throat. He will, he realises, have to carry this old man until one of them dies. Probably Sinbad. Then the old man will go on to find some other youngster to perch on. Our hero releases himself by getting the old man drunk. In some versions, he kills him.

The institutions of marriage and the nuclear family, which used to supply terminal comfort for their old relatives on their way out of the world, are melting away. For the first time in 2016, more couples were co-habiting in loose, unsolemnised long-term union than were taking 'vows' – ecclesiastic or secular.

Middle-class women (particularly) who find themselves 'sandwiched' – looking after children and incapacitated parents – are increasingly resentful and unwilling to assume these Sinbadian burdens. Especially single mothers – of whom there are an increasing number. It takes a village to raise a child as the title of Hillary Clinton's pious treatise had it. Where, nowadays, is the 'village' to look after the old? The hospital, of course. Or, as they are now called, 'trusts'.

The build-up of undischargeable old patients in hospitals creates a condition of institutional sclerosis. The solution is obvious, but too expensive to contemplate. An aggressive hospice-building programme and generously funded long-term care communities would unclog the NHS. But the costs of converting the UK into the world's largest old folks' home are unthinkable.

House-Hoarding and Wealth Accumulation

The house-hoarding issue is different from bed-blocking and is directed against the middle-class elderly who have defied the Reaper long enough to pay off their 25-year mortgages (literally 'death-trusts').

The UK's unimaginably vast wealth is buried – like Silas Marner's gold – under the nation's floorboards. Literally. The ancient dragon Smaug, in *The Hobbit*, sitting on a mountain of inert, excremental gold, might be the better literary analogy than George Eliot's (died aged 61) Weaver of Raveloe.

This wholly notional wealth, essentially the value of British bricks and mortar, amounts to mind-boggling trillions. Nine trillion at the time of writing. The chips can't be cashed in, of course. The system would implode, creating that dreaded Victorian thing, a 'run' on the banks (one is told that, in 2008, the ATM machines were minutes from monetary depletion).

The nine trillions are as notional as Monopoly's Bank of Fun money. Or the Zimbabwean $100 trillion banknote, more useful as toilet paper than currency.

Wise economists inform me that a minimally exact 3 per cent of the under-the-floorboards trillions has to be released as hard cash every year to keep the economy's wheels turning. But consider this: if house-hoarding oldies are living longer (twenty years longer, on average, if we go back to my childhood) and not selling up, that necessary 3 per cent lubricant is trapped in a condition of fiscal constipation. Like Smaug, the old won't do the decent thing and get off the golden pot.

As my dismal economist friend told me, 2008 was merely a fore-tremor of what's on its way. Unless, he added grimly, 'something is done'. What adds fuel to the oncoming fire is the fact that the vast (and wholly notional) under-floorboard wealth has, to keep the great ship of state afloat, to rise absurdly in value (so-called), until houses are unaffordable. At least to the young first-time buyer.

The ideal adjustment would be a return to the rational lifespans – e.g. the biblical 'threescore years and ten' – of the 1960s, when the 'golden cascade', as John Major called it, ran strong between the generations, when life expectancy was up to twenty years less and when houses were, for the average first-time purchaser, between two and five times the annual middle-class income. Happy days. I remember them well.

The basic problem is that we are living, as a nation, beyond our means and, to repeat the point, beyond our traditional lifespans. The solution is not, as is often suggested, for oldsters to 'trade down', vacating their houses for their young move in, like so many young hermit crabs, but for the British economy, in toto, to come to its senses and embark on a social housing project before apocalypse. One fears it won't. Rationality would lose too many votes. Low-intensity war is easier.

The Machinery of Death

The Nazis, during their *totale krieg*, perfected two ways of disposing of what their filthy ideology defined as obstructive human waste. One, a triumph of perverse bureaucracy and advanced genocidal technology, was the concentration camp.

For the millions of (mainly Russian) prisoners of war the Wehrmacht had scooped up in their triumphant 1941 invasion into the USSR, the alternative Nazi solution was enclosure behind barbed wire, and total neglect. Deliberate privation and starvation, well out of sight, was the principal policy for those luckless Slav *untermenschen*. Cannibalism was rife. Death was inevitable. Close on 57 per cent (four million) of those imprisoned perished in the *Russenlager*. Problem solved costlessly – on with the war.

Negligence, as perfected by the Nazis, had become a weapon of mass destruction. Killing was too expensive. It cost a bullet and needed a man away from the front line to fire it.

'Care' Homes

In an old fable a grandfather, in the clumsiness of age,
is constantly breaking crockery. His family give him a
wooden plate. They later see a child carving a piece of
timber. 'What are you making?' they ask. 'A wooden
plate for you when you get old,' the child replies.

In the UK, 'care', as it's euphemistically called (as misleading an epithet as 'concentration' in concentration
camp'),[12] is farmed out to profiteers.

The new camps for the new Ancient Brits are called
'care homes'. On offer for around £35–60k annually, these warehouses are (far too many of them, one
deduces) neither care-giving nor homely. They oper-
ate, however, with the efficiency of lemon squeezers to
extract what they want.

Care homes are, the worst of them, a machinery
which 'efficiently' (a key word in this context) takes
care of an otherwise intractable social problem while

---

12   Martin Amis makes amusing play with the Nazi love of evasive euphemism
for horror in his most recent novel, *Zone of Interest*.

stuffing speculators' pockets and enabling local authorities to boast that they have 'sorted' the problem of what to do with Father William.[13]

The fundamental question the care industry raises is contentious: can you privatise family love? An answer, for modern times, is given in the case of the Southern Cross debacle.

The Rise and Fall of Southern Cross

No one gets out of here alive.

– JIM MORRISON (DIED AGED 27)

At its height in the early years of the century, Southern Cross owned and managed 750 care homes, employing

---

13 For those who miss the allusion, Lewis Carroll's nonsense poem:
'You are old, Father William,' the young man said,
'And your hair has become very white;
And yet you incessantly stand on your head –
Do you think, at your age, it is right?'

44,000 workers providing for 31,000 superannuated residents.[14]

The firm began as a go-getter enterprise in the mid-1990s. Its wily originators saw a profitable opening. Local authorities would pay good money to have a tricky social care problem taken off their hands. There was plenty of good money swilling around then. Times were good. Problems, specifically the provision of care for the declining population, without old-fashioned families to support them, could be buried in wads of public cash. A sizeable wad of which could be extracted from the aged customers themselves, if they were house-owners and had thriftily amassed savings.

Business expertise, know-how and a flashy display of 'five-star' *equipage* made Southern Cross an attractive service provider once they had established themselves as the market leader. Their major asset was selling themselves. Their expensive services were brochure-led. Payment for Southern Cross 'care' was,

---

14 In the paragraphs which follow I am informed by, and quote, Richard Wachman's account in *The Guardian*, 16 July 2011.

in some cases, borne by the patient supplemented by the local council, or entirely by the council.[15]

One of Southern Care's cannier practices was to convert large salubrious country houses – cheaply acquired and distant enough to inhibit families dropping by too often to visit or, perish the thought, co-reside with their loved ones. The formula was a winner. As Richard Wachman reports: 'By 2003, the company owned more than 100 homes and was attracting the attention of investment bankers. "You could see the firm was going places – management was ambitious and as it grew, so did the financial returns," said [a] former executive.'

No mention, of course, as to whether the interests of the residents were being served. It was a money machine and a social convenience.

In 2004, the US private equity group (i.e. hedge fund) Blackstone (grand masters of 'alternative assets management') acquired Southern Cross for £167 million. They converted it into a money pump, with a wickedly clever

---

15 There was recurrent irritation about the unfairness of the 'means-testing'. Why save thriftily all your life, it was asked, when the more feckless got the same treatment as you free of charge?

stroke of financial legerdemain. Wachman explains how it worked and how, eventually and disastrously, it could never work:

> Ludicrously, as it turned out, Blackstone supported a sale-and-leaseback business model that was all too common at the time.
>
> Under this system, Southern Cross's operating company and property assets were separated. It was blatant financial engineering but it made sense on paper: acquisitions could be financed by spinning off the bricks and mortar into a different company, selling it on to property investors and then using the proceeds to buy more care operators.

It was creating debt to create profit with the expectation, against the immutable laws of mathematical economics, that the latter could permanently outstrip the former. It was classic pyramidism and bubble, with some smoke and mirrors, supplied by Southern Cross publicity, to attract the punters. Property values were soaring and interest rates were low. And, of course, the market (sick old people) was, with longevity, ever increasing. And most local councils were suckers. It couldn't go wrong.

Nor, in the boom years, did it. Southern Cross (preposterous name) was able to place one card on top of another to create an empire. Councils liked what the glossy new firm was offering. Most particularly its 'look'. Southern Cross put a lot of effort into that side of things. But, behind the glossy façade, leaseback had locked the firm into paying hefty, incrementally increasing, rents for their network of homes, along with high-interest mortgages for the new properties they were acquiring. Costs were necessarily cut (call it 'efficiency'), particularly in the quality of staff and basic creature comforts (such as, one might fantasise, a fresh glass of water by the bed, clean sheets, bathing; little cuttable things of that kind).

Things jogged along, expansively and remuneratively, until 2008, when the epochal 'crash' torpedoed property values and paralysed the market. The rents and mortgages they had contracted for were now a noose around the firm's neck. Southern Cross had, ingeniously, woven a rope to hang itself with.

Blackstone were gone by 2006. They were not

long-term cash investors. They left with £1.1 billion in their pockets (this at a time when the pound was 'high') and went on to happily hedge elsewhere. They were good at what they did. Rural British care homes had worked very well for Blackstone. Whether or not it produced the best care for the poor people lodging under the Southern Cross roof was something else. It hadn't, of course; but that was not the point.

Councils, who were similarly hit below the water line by the post-2008 crisis, suddenly found, abracadabra, they could save money by the 'efficiency' of meals on wheels and fly-by, minimum-wage, peripatetic carers (some of whom stayed only minutes, gabbling merrily in foreign tongues) until the old people's condition they cared for was terminal and the local hospitals' problem.

What these 'fleeting visits' typically meant was, it was revealed years later, as follows:

> Care minister Norman Lamb has called for a 'fundamental' overhaul of home help services, after an investigation exposed more than half a million visits that lasted less than five minutes each.

New figures, obtained under the Freedom of Information Act, show rising numbers of council checks on the elderly and disabled are taking place in a matter of minutes.

Charities have raised fears that vulnerable pensioners are being neglected and are being forced to choose between being washed or fed.

Ministers have repeatedly pledged to crack down on the scandal of 'clock-watch care' by services contracted to councils [to] provide visits of 15 minutes or less.[16]

Fifteen minutes. 'Or less'.

Southern Cross found themselves in the years following the 2008 crash no longer running the happy communities for the 'active aged' portrayed glossily in their advertising material doing the rhumba or pilates. Their homes were increasingly dumping grounds for the incurably demented, comatose and incontinent who could not be dealt with by the Speedy Gonzalez

---

16 Laura Donnelly, *Daily Telegraph*, 15 February 2015.

five-minute council carers. It was a mess and getting messier all the time.

Southern Cross, those with a historical cast of mind might think, was being redefined by iron financial imperatives (particularly those damned rents) into creating a modern version of the Victorian workhouse. Where was the modern Dickens, or Mrs Gaskell, when you needed them?

Random offences were 'exposed' with increasing frequency by investigative reporters. 'Lessons were learned', as the routine sidestep put it. A rotten apple or so was tossed self-righteously out of the barrel. But the substantive fact was clear as day. 'Market forces' could, in fat years, make pots of money in the provision of half-decent 'home care', but not in lean years, when, like Southern Cross, you might end up without a pot to piss in.

The privatised home care system couldn't, by its nature, privatise what – since time immemorial – families have provided free of charge. TLC (tender loving care). The agencies of regulation that had been set up did not properly regulate, or regulate with sufficient severity. The Care Quality Commission (absurd name) sniffily inspected and issued improvement orders by the score to Southern Care homes. They were either fooled or self-fooled, it later emerged, as to what was actually going on.

Other large cohorts of the population who felt they were getting a raw deal – students infuriated by university fees, for example – could take to the streets – violently, on occasion, when their youthful dander was really up. The old, infirm and terminally decayed could only suffer quietly as they waited for someone to kindly take them to the lavatory or bring a glass of water. Or be nice to them.

The rottenness at the core of the pre-2011 Southern Cross, and the factory-scale abuse of the old the system promulgated, was exposed to public view in the symptomatic case of Orchid View, in Copthorne, West Sussex. The home opened in 2009 as a 'state of the art' establishment, worth every penny of the £3,000 per month charge it levied from the council or better-off customers. What that 'art' meant came to light in late 2011, when Southern Cross collapsed into a steaming, debt-ridden heap.

What had been going on was not a particularly

well-kept secret. Whistle blowers had blown their whis-
tles – one had actually informed on the iniquities of the
place to the police, who dropped by, tut-tutted and did
nothing.

The 'final straw' for this whistle blower was when
she learned that twenty-eight cases of faulty medication
had been dispensed on one night shift alone. 'Do what
you like,' she was apparently instructed.

One luckless Orchid View victim was grossly over-
dosed, an inquest was later informed, with warfarin
– famous elsewhere as rat poison – for three whole weeks
before her frail body gave up the unequal struggle.
The 'home manager' was alleged to have instructed
that the relevant documents be shredded to cover up the
overdose, and new documents created. The instruction
(allegedly) was accompanied by the graphic observation:
'Shit, we can't send her to hospital with those. They will
shut us down.' That, not the deaths of residents, would
be the real disaster.

Orchid View was a deadly place to end your days.
'Abandon all hope ye who enter here' could well have
been inscribed over its pretty, vined entrance. Up to

nineteen patients (a bulk of the residents) died in what were initially thought to be suspicious circumstances. They were neglected to death, it was alleged. It was a furtive massacre, particularly hard to prove in court. Inmates were mistreated, kept alive until 'natural causes' (malnutrition, dehydration, 'misapplication of medicine') could be held at bay no longer and the paying customer went, finally, to the welcome relief offered by the undertaker and grave-digger.

The way the 'home' operated was wrenched out, grudgingly, from a mass of obfuscating records at subsequent inquests and ponderous commissions of review. Vignettes of miscare so extreme as to verge on the sadistic emerged. A Boots medical supplier was so disgusted by what she saw behind the walls of Orchid View, she reportedly vomited in the car park.

A 77-year-old patient, writhing in agony, naked on soiled sheets, was tangled in her catheter. A family member reportedly found staff eating toast in their room nearby, drinking tea with their feet up. When she asked that something be done, the family member was blandly informed: 'Everyone is entitled to a break.' A patient's broken ankle (and the agony it mutely caused) was over-looked for days. These were fragmentary glimpses of the way Orchid View – routinely, one could plausibly assume – operated.

The home was, the inquest on the victims of Orchid View care later declared, worm-holed with 'institutional abuse' – a mealy-mouthed description of what was actually going on in the place. And precisely which 'institution' was doing the abusing? Southern Cross itself? The local West Sussex Council who employed their services? The manager and staff at Orchid View? Britain, in its national indifference, verging on hostility, to how its old people were treated? That last, I'd suggest.

One thing was clear as day. Money had been made, in pots, by Southern Cross in the years before 2008. But not enough money had been put into doing what Southern Cross's advertisements brashly promised it would do. And too much loot had been siphoned out. A billion pounds of it was now across the Atlantic, being invested elsewhere.

That siphoning was one salient fact. Another was that so long as it could all be kept out of sight, no one (other than the families visiting, and the occasional vomiting saleswoman in the car park) gave a sweet damn. Old people die. And, while they are going downhill, money can be made out of them. The old people weren't happy with what their money got? Caveat emptor. But old people can't, unlike car buyers, shop around until they find the deal that suits them.

Starve a dog to death, and the long arm of the law will come down on you like a ton of bricks. Neglect an old person to death and, it would seem, you are free to go on and practise your callousness elsewhere, with the skills you have picked up in the last job. Some of the Orchid View staff did, apparently, do just that. Indeed, the 'area manager', according to *The Argus*, didn't even have to take the trouble of moving on elsewhere, but was re-employed as the 'regional manager'.

Incredibly, the Care Quality Commission (CQC) had given the home a 'good', two-star rating in 2010, a year before it closed down in a welter of inmate mistreatment.

The routine, all-round defence positions were assumed, with the full barrage of stale metaphor. 'Lessons' had been 'learned' (was killing old people something 'educational'?), 'root-and-branch' investigations would be launched (this was agricultural?). Orchid View was, it was protested, an 'isolated' example. The single rotten apple. Other residents in other Southern Cross places were as happy as sandboys, one was led to believe.

At the final day of the five-week inquest into the deaths of the nineteen elderly Orchid View residents, which were mysteriously inexplicable, the coroner could punitively indict no one and nothing. Apparently what happened to old people in Orchid View was not an easily defined felonious offence. It was inefficiency. Call it 'sub-optimal care' and make sure it doesn't happen again was the answer.

The coroner concluded: 'It's a heartbreaking case. We all have parents who will probably need care in the latter part of their lives.' God prevent they end up in places like Orchid View.

With a new name and management, under a new regime, Orchid View was re-opened. The new name was not, as far as I can make out, publicised. It would be as unsaleable, with that can tied to its tail, as the Amityville horror house. The manager who had been in charge at the height of the scandal was belatedly struck off in 2015.

What conclusions can one draw? The Southern Cross financial debacle and the horrors of Orchid View were symptomatic of a larger, pervasive attitude to old people. It was rooted in the sense that they were not actually people at all but a socio-economic 'problem'. Something, that is, to be erased while no one was looking.

Except, perhaps, some nosy newspaper. The print newspaper industry is in a bad way, one is told. Circulations are falling. God help England if, as is threatened, newspapers (national and local) go under.

Constructive Negligence

Exterminate the brutes.

– KURTZ'S DESPAIRING CONCLUSION IN CONRAD'S
HEART OF DARKNESS

In the UK's current care programmes for the old, one needs no digital hearing aid (wonderful invention) to catch faint echoes of the Dalek's 'Exterminate! Exterminate! Exterminate!' in the *Doctor Who* TV saga. On 2 May 2016, the *Telegraph*'s lead story ('exclusive') was that:

As many as 40,000 patients a year are having 'do not resuscitate' orders secretly imposed on them without their families ever being told, it can be disclosed.

A national audit of dying patients has highlighted a failure by authorities to tell relatives of plans put in place for their loved ones.

It is estimated that every year, more than 200,000 patients are issued with do not resuscitate orders, instructing doctors not to attempt cardiopulmonary resuscitation if the patient suffers a cardiac arrest or stops breathing.

The official audit of 9,000 dying patients, conducted by the Royal College of Physicians, reveals that one-in-five families were not informed that a 'do not resuscitate' order had been put in place – equivalent to the families of 40,000 patients.

The same study showed that in 16 per cent of cases, there was no record of a conversation with the dying

patient, or explanation for the lack of one, for the
decision to put in place a do not resuscitate order.[17]

Forty thousand a year is a figure at which a WWI Field
Marshal would look twice.

The DNR mass-labelling may well be based on
'rational' white-coat decision-making and a 'must be
cruel only to be kind' resolve. But it is the underlying
attitude, and tell-tale secrecy (it had to be uncovered
and 'exposed' to be known about), that is instructive.
The trusts (misleading name) did not, clearly, want this
death-sentencing practice to 'come out'. What one per-
ceives in this DNR mass-labelling is not 'care' of the old,
but a waste disposal exercise – done discreetly, hopefully with no one looking. Or caring.

One can boil the blood by doing a search, any day
of the week, on 'elderly abuse' on Google News.
Heart-rending stories abound there and in the daily
newspapers – particularly in the *Daily Mail* (average
reader's age 58 years), which, to its credit (or perhaps

---

17 The article is credited to the *Telegraph*'s Health Editor, Laura Donnelly.
Good on her, say I.

the initiative of its editor, Paul Dacre, age 67), launched a 'Dignity for the Elderly' campaign in 2010.

Dignity? Cruelly parched elderly patients are described emptying the sour dregs of flower vases by their beds to quench their agonising thirst; they are verbally abused for wetting beds, like miscreant puppies, by 'nurses', so-called, jabbering scornfully in languages their patients don't understand; robbed of wedding rings (they won't need them where they're going). These are anecdotes I have read about, heard about, and believe. Occasionally, as I say, they are confirmed by clandestine cameras installed by suspicious families.

These extreme delinquencies are by no means universal. But they are common enough to symbolise a tolerated heartlessness at work. Perhaps, one can go on to surmise, an officially undiscouraged attitude. There is someone, somewhere, who could stop it, but doesn't quite get round to doing it.

Just yesterday, as I write, there was a front-page story in the *Daily Mail* (28 July 2016) about cataracts. It's a lovely word: one recalls waterfalls in faraway places. In medical parlance it describes eyeballs glazing over as if, as one *Mail* informant put it, some gremlin were coming every night and smearing them with Vaseline.

Cataracts are one of the commoner woes age is heir to, and verging on universal if you are lucky enough to live long enough and spend a lot of time in sunlight. I'm pre-cataractic by having spent much of my life in southern California, scorning the Ray-Bans my friends wore. It is not a big thing medically. Cataract opacity can be remedied by a routine laser and lens replacement operation.[18]

The operation is not expensive. The results are beyond dramatic. As one recipient told me, wonderingly, after her operation it was as if the world changed from black and white to Technicolor (she had waited two years for her second eye to be done). A national crash programme could wholly eradicate cataracts in the aged in a trice and make a lot of old people happy (and safer drivers).

The front-page story, the result of *Mail* research (i.e. phone calls) and Freedom of Information digging (by

---

18 It can't be done under general anaesthetic: in the olden days, seeing the scalpel approach, as Samson saw the Philistine red-hot poker, must have required iron nerve.

some enterprising interns, probably), discovered (it's worth quoting at length):

> Three-quarters of hospitals are denying the elderly life-changing cataract operations until they have all but lost their sight...
>
> Health trusts are refusing to offer the surgery unless a patient's vision is so poor they cannot read large letters displayed on a wall – with glasses.
>
> Even then, some trusts only refer patients for surgery if they have fallen twice in the last year, also have hearing problems, care for a loved one, or live alone.
>
> The life-transforming procedure costs less than £1,000 per eye – yet it is being rationed by NHS managers so that even those in direst need are being subjected to humiliating tests and form-filling exercises.
>
> More than half of over-65s, some 4.5 million individuals, suffer from cataracts to some degree. They occur when the lens in the eye becomes cloudy with age.
>
> But campaigners say thousands of patients are now losing their sight and being condemned to misery because the NHS won't treat them until they are nearly blind.

To make matters worse, it has emerged that some foreign health tourists have been able to jump the queue for the surgery. An investigation using Freedom of Information requests today reveals:

- Seventy-three per cent of hospitals have imposed strict guidelines which determine only those worst-affected by the condition are treated,
- Patients must fail a sight test when wearing glasses and sometimes also prove they cannot work, read or recognise loved ones,
- In some instances, they have to fill out a form, ticking whether they have fallen over, live alone or care for a loved one,
- Half of hospitals will only do the worst-affected eye. Patients are told they only need to see out of one,
- Waiting times for those who are allowed the operation are up to a year and a half.

Cataracts get worse with time and some victims are so severely affected they cannot read, watch TV, recognise faces or drive.

> But the condition is easily treatable with a 30-minute
> operation to remove the cloudy lens and replace it with
> a plastic implant.[19]

What the *Mail* uncovers in this story is institutionally, NHS-wide, licensed negligence and indifference
to the suffering of the old. A decision has been taken to
put the money elsewhere. With luck, the aged cataract
sufferer may die – or fall terminally ill – before their
number comes up, in eighteen months or whatever after
diagnosis.

Doing Anything to Avoid Doing Something

'Do anything to avoid doing something.' The motto
should be inscribed in brass and stuck over the door
of No. 10 (along with 'We're all living longer, which is
a good thing'). It's an automatic response to problems
which are intractable, long-term, expensive, vote-losers,

---

19 The story is credited to Sophie Borland and Josh White.

or merely awkward. Policies affecting care and respect for the old come into all those categories. Politicians demonstrate the nimble footwork of a Wayne Rooney kicking the problems into the long grass.

Consider, for example, the following editorial from the *Mail* (6 January 2012), picking up on its own front-page splash that day, under the headline 'Neglect on the Wards':

> Having been appalled by cases of the elderly being left to starve on NHS wards, David Cameron yesterday demanded huge improvements in the standard of care provided by nurses, who will be instructed to speak to their patients at least once an hour.
>
> We welcome his insistence that nursing 'needs to be about patients not paperwork.' But it's deeply depressing that it requires a direct order from the Prime Minister for patients to be treated with the basic humanity which should be guaranteed in any civilised society.[20]

---

20 I'm aware that I'm drawing heavily on the *Mail*, here and elsewhere. It is not, to be candid, a paper I agree with politically. But its 'Dignity for the Old' commitment has made it peerless in reporting on what interests me in this book.

It's an exemplary case of seeming to engage with a problem while nimbly side-stepping it. If, as persuasively reported by the *Mail*, 'the elderly are being left to starve' (Starve? Who says this isn't war?) in NHS 'care', the 'huge improvement', surely, would be to feed the poor old sods with whatever gruel was going, not look at them every hour as they fade meekly into inanition. That, however, would cost money (in the following week, another story reported that trusts were spending as little as 94 pence on patients' meals. *Bon appétit*).

Requiring that a box be ticked, recording that the patient has been spoken to 'at least once an hour' (during their sleep?) was costless. And, of course, filled no stomach. But in what language would that hourly speaking be done? In the same paper, which congratulated the PM, there was another story, on 14 January 2012, headlined '90% of Hospitals Fail to Check on Nurses' English before Letting Them Work on Wards'.

EU regulations, apparently, forbade discriminating against otherwise professionally qualified overseas applicants on the eligibility ground that they had insufficient command of the English language.[21]

A chronic shortage of home-grown 'nurse-assistant' recruits into the nursing profession meant that they had to be imported from overseas – like the mythic Polish plumber.

It is easier to explain by sign language to a monoglot Pole that your ballcock is defective than to explain to a monoglot Eastern European nurse (however sympathetic) that something is going wrong with your thorax. The *Mail* quoted, by way of illustration, the experience of one old(ish), witty patient:

> Jan Middleton … said she nearly had to call 999 and summon paramedics to her hospital ward because nurses could not understand her.

---

21 This is a somewhat tangled area. The UK's first, not entirely satisfactory, attempt to circumvent the EU rules was to test outside the Community area. Over the period 2014/15, stricter rules were brought in. But the fact remains that there was a serious language deficit – particularly with older patients, where communication can mean life or death. For a résumé of the issue see https://www.nursingtimes.net/roles/nurse-managers/new-english-language-test-agreed-for-european-nurses/5091001.article.

The former lawyer was recovering from emergency surgery for a brain infection at Charing Cross Hospital in London when she woke in the middle of the night and found that the wound had become infected.

She repeatedly tried to explain to the only nurse on duty that she urgently needed to see a doctor, but the nurse could not understand her.

The 54-year-old said, 'I was getting very, very distressed and in quite a panic. Which is why in the end I said 'I'm dialling 999 for an ambulance'.

It is pure theatre of the absurd. An ambulance, klaxon wailing, lights flashing, rushes to the hospital, with a dictionary on board. Ms Middleton's uncomprehending nurses, she said, were from Eastern Europe and Asia. The hospital responded that it would in future pay more attention to the communication ability of recruits from abroad. In passing, one may note that, at 54 years of age, Ms Middleton was a relatively young old person. What if she had been 84 and in similar straits?

Unsurprisingly, this state of affairs, dealing with nurses who might as well have been Klingons, is particularly irking for the old. As Katherine Murphy, chief executive of the Patients Association, told the paper: 'We get a lot of calls from relatives saying elderly patients are trying to ask for more pain relief or that they want something different to eat and the message just isn't getting across. Often these patients who are physically very weak just give up.'

At-Home Care

In July 2015, Age Concern issued the following dire bulletin on Britain's 'care' for its elderly:

> The state of elderly care in England is 'unacceptable in a civilised society', the country's leading charity representing older people said, as figures reveal more than a million now get no help at all for basic care.
>
> Age UK said swingeing cuts to social care budgets under the coalition, combined with a growing elderly population, had led to an 'exponential' increase in the number of people left to struggle alone.
>
> For the first time, Age UK said, more than a million

have a care need – such as getting out of bed, going to the toilet, preparing food or taking medication – but receive no help from the state, self-funded care services, or from friends, family or neighbours.

The charity said 1,004,000 people fall into this category – an increase of more than 100,000 in the past year.

And growing by the hundreds of thousands every year. Money would solve it in no time, of course. But purse strings, in the form of government funds released to local authorities, are being drawn throttlingly tight. 'Don't care: do less. Above all, don't let the *Daily Mail* or *The Sun* get hold of the story' is the covert message behind so-called care policy. Call it un-care. Officially sanctioned. Let the old sods soil their underpants.

I repeat the point I'm making, ad nauseam, in this book. Malpractice, outright abuse and thoughtless neglect are so widespread, and so winked at, as to suggest at best covertly sanctioned indifference and at worst a clandestine 'policy' – constructive negligence. Deliberate un-care. The larger aim would seem to be disposal: placing state responsibility for the old (eight million over 70 by 2020 – twice the population of Norway) on a back burner so far back no one sees. After all, there are no votes in it. Many of the demented, bedridden and disabled could not even make it to the booth or remember who it was they intended to vote for.

Part III

Final Solutions

There'll be a population of demented very old people, like an invasion of terrible immigrants stinking out the restaurants and cafés and shops ... I can imagine a sort of civil war between the old and the young in 10 or 15 years' time. There should be a booth on every corner where you could get a martini and a medal.

– MARTIN AMIS ON THE EUTHANASIATIC FUTURE AWAITING US, IN AN INTERVIEW WITH THE *SUNDAY TIMES*, 24 JANUARY 2010

A N INCREASINGLY TEMPTING, if gothic, solution is what Martin Amis, our glum Diogenes (once our *enfant terrible*), foresees; Necropolis. In a few years' time, Martin predicts, there will be a *cabinet d'euthanasie* on every street.[22] *End-lösung*, as the Nazis called it (final solution).

For those well-thinking oldies of the future who duti-fully check into the euthanasia sheds, but never check out (like the famed Roach Motel, in the US), there should be a free martini ('last drinks, please') and a medal, Amis whimsically suggests. And welcome darkness. The same darkness from which we came into the world.

There will, for a certainty, be a relaxation on 'self-murder', as the Christian church used to call it, over the next few years. Bet on it. No more Swiss final-des-tination trips will be required. 'Final Exit' (the title of Derek Humphry's DIY 'assisted death' manual) will be provided in the 'home' country. Perhaps, even, the state of the art 'suicide sacks' and helium (the latest suicide machinery: look it up on the web) will be distributed on the NHS. Forget martinis and medals.

There are, as the father of sociology, Émile Dur-kheim, argued in his classic analysis, three types of suicide: *anomic* (rootlessness, nothing to live for);

---

22 Where the public urinals used to be, perhaps, before the councils discovered they were too expensive to provide.

egoistic (personal reasons; e.g. my dog died); *altruis-tic* (as in war – you 'give your life' for your country or your 'cause'; for something more important, as you decide, than your own meagre existence).

What we need now, it could be argued, is a new, post-Durkheimian, cult of altruistic suicide, not pro bono publico but pro bono juvenium. Or so juvenium thinks. Till then we'll have to make do with covert triage (see the above on DNR). And, for those of a pilgrim con-stitution, the final, one-way, journey to Dignitas. I have a friend who, more frugally, keeps a jug of oramorph, held over from her dead husband's last months, along-side the skimmed milk for self-disposal. But, as the film *Still Alice* suggests, what if you can't remember, when you need it, where you hid it? Every war, as that eleventh day in November reminds us, has those heroes who give up their lives for what they believe is greater than them-selves. Why should the old not do the same? Pro patria.

There is, however, an interesting and rather hopeful counter-current. It relates, yet again, to the trend-setting, inextinguishably contrarian, baby boomers. On 4 March 2015, the BBC reported:

Once elderly people in the UK were the most likely group to take their own lives, but now they are at lower risk than the middle-aged. Why? ... The latest figures from the UK's Office for National Statistics (ONS) show middle-aged men are the most likely group to do so, the suicide rate among them having risen to its highest level since the early 1980s.

But something mentioned less often is that, over a longer period, the number of elderly people in the UK killing themselves has fallen massively.

In the early 1930s, the height of the Great Depression, as many as 50 per 100,000 men over the age of 65 took their lives every year in England and Wales. After a slump during World War Two, the figure was back up to above 40 in the late 1950s, making the elderly the most at-risk group.

But the suicide rate declined sharply during the 1960s and early 1970s. It plateaued into the 1980s and then fell again from the end of that decade.

The latest ONS figures, for the whole UK in 2013, show the suicide rate among men aged 60 to 74 was 14.5 per 100,000 and 15.4 for those aged 75 and over. For women of the same ages, the figures are 3.9 and 4.7 per

100,000, roughly a quarter of the rates of the late 1950s and mid-1960s.

For both sexes the elderly are now the least likely to kill themselves, apart from 15–29-year-olds.

Those baby boomers. Always changing the rules.

Even as the darkness approaches they can always squeeze more out of life and living than any generation before them. And, quite feasibly, any generation after them.

Little Things Mean a Lot

One of the oddities of the war on the old is the use by the other side of trivia, inflated, nonsensically, into issues of absurdly major significance. For example, the following four casus bellis (I believe that is the plural):

1. The free bus pass
2. The winter fuel allowance
3. The over-75 free TV licence
4. The triple-lock pension guarantee

One should note, in passing, that the 'free prescriptions' from which the old benefit at close on £9 a shot do not enrage anyone. Even though they are genuinely expensive to the public purse. Why not? Because, unlike the above quartet, they are widely distributed among the less than old. Exemptions from prescription charge cover, as the regulations pedantically specify:

> Children under 16, pregnant women, people over 60, young people in full-time education, people in receipt of certain benefits such as Income Support or Jobseekers' Allowance and people suffering from specific conditions, such as certain types of physical disability, diabetes, or epilepsy, for which they hold a valid exemption certificate.

In Northern Ireland, Wales and Scotland, the charges have been abolished altogether.

The Curious Case of the Millionaire's Bus Pass

On 5 December 2011, on the BBC *Today* programme (listenership between two and three million on the first 8 o/c slot), Nick Clegg (aged 44 then, 49 now), the Deputy PM, as he then was, delivered himself of the sage view that 'we should be asking *millionaire pensioners* to perhaps make a little sacrifice on their free TV licence or their free bus passes'.

In subsequent comments he pointed out that 12 million Britons, no less, qualified for the 'free' bus pass. Meanwhile, free TV licences for the over-75s ['them'], introduced by the last Labour government, 'cost the country [i.e. 'us', the Cleggs of England] £550 million a year'. Clegg's comment and statistics were picked up and kicked around for a day or two by every news outlet.

Our national generosity to the old was ruining us. What on earth were 'we' thinking of? These were universal benefits. Not, if one gave it a moment's thought, because anyone thought they were useful outside

metropolitan areas,[23] but because means-testing is
(1) expensive; and (2) electoral suicide.

The case can easily be made that the bus pass liber-
ates the old who no longer trust themselves to drive and
cannot afford Uber. But the logical flaw is in Clegg's
preposterous epithet 'millionaire'. 'Millionaire pensioners' belong in the mythical bestiary along with unicorns,
mermaids and Roswell aliens.

Speaking personally, I don't often find myself plunked
alongside Alan Sugar on my London Transport 88
double-decker to north Camden. And, of course, if bus
passes aren't used, or applied for, they cost the country
nothing. Do the Prince of Wales, or Sir Mick Jagger –
both of whom qualify (and are millionaires many times
over) – bother to stand at line in their local municipal
office to pick up their passes?

Moreover, as was wearily pointed out, means-testing
pensioners to identify those free-loading millionaires using
my 88 bus to get to their lunch at the Ritz would cost
more than any revenue that could conceivably be saved.

---

23 Try waiting for a bus in Little Bogwallow on the Marsh.

Clegg's comment (he mischievously repeated it over the following weeks) kicked up the desired swirls of dust. Two days later, on 7 December, Benedict Brogan in the *Telegraph* chipped in on cue with a column headlined 'David Cameron Shouldn't Be Afraid to Ask Pensioners to Do Their Bit'. Their 'bit'? Dim recollections of Vera Lynn were evoked. The article was subtitled: 'The elderly are entitled to such lavish benefits that accepting a little less wouldn't be hard'. *Lavish*? The article continued in the same miserly vein:

> In this age of austerity, we are in danger of upending the process. On the Government's present trajectory, a younger generation, hit with falling incomes and a lower standard of living than the one its parents enjoyed, will be required to prop up sumptuous entitlements for pensioners who made it good before it all went wrong...
>
> Why, some on the Right ask, should the state reward longevity when money would be better spent helping those who need it? Do old people deserve to watch telly more than the disabled? Is heating more expensive for grandparents than it is for single mums?

The *Telegraph* – doorstep-delivered copies of which should come wrapped in a Barbour jacket when it rains – posing as the paper for 'single mums' is a bit of a stretch.

Having reneged on their 'pledge' on student fees (which they could, in the coalition, have resisted), the Lib Dems were vengefully decimated in the 2015 election and Clegg (no longer required by the Tories as deputy leader) resigned as leader of his party.

There was, however, an interesting follow-up. Clegg's usefulness to the Conservatives in the years of the coalition was rewarded. On 24 July 2016, Laura Hughes, political correspondent of the *Telegraph*, reported:

Nick Clegg has been granted an expenses allowance worth up to £115,000 a year that was previously only awarded to former prime ministers, it has emerged.

The former deputy prime minister and Liberal Democrat leader claimed £101,911 from the so-called public duty cost allowance last year.

The grant, which is reviewed annually, has traditionally

been granted to former leaders to help cover the costs related to their public duties.

It comes on top of thousands of pounds of earnings Mr Clegg has made giving private speeches, including £22,500 for a two-and-a-half hour session for the bank Goldman Sachs.

Is Mr Clegg a millionaire? The quality of his neckties suggests he is. Thank heavens the currently meaningless senior politician (as he once was) won't have to dig into his Savile Row pockets for a £1.50 bus ticket, while he waits a dozen years for his bus pass.

The 'Ridiculous' Home Heating Allowance

In *The Times* (average age of readers: a ball-park 60), Hugo Rifkind (age 39) wrote an opinion piece on 19 July 2016 fulsomely entitled: 'The plight of the young is a problem for all of us: the blatant advantages in wealth for baby boomers will lead to a damaging breakdown in trust between generations'.

The article opened, all guns blazing:

It's surprisingly easy to offend baby boomers. After reading just that one sentence, I bet a whole bunch of them are offended already. Sure, they might not do petitions, or Twitter hashtag campaigns, or demand 'safe spaces' from people vile and crass enough to assume they're probably female just because they're wearing a frock and a ponytail and are called Emily. You just try, though, telling somebody born between the Second World War and the mid-1960s that they might have had an easier life than somebody a bit younger. Meltdown. They make Generation Snowflake look positively stoical. 'We worked hard!' they'll shout, from their massive houses which cost them a whole two years' salary in 1976. 'And we didn't have iPhones!'

The occasion for the piece, and Rifkind's belligerent satire and rather cheap cracks about iPhones, was twofold. First was a report from a think tank (there are more of them around than at the battle of Kursk, nowadays) which had discovered a 'fraying contract between the generations'.

Second was the calendrical fact that

> If the baby boom began in 1946, the oldest baby boomers
> are today turning 70. While this cohort was in the prime of
> its working life, being old was, indeed, a decent indicator
> of being poor, too. This is why pensioners today get travel
> discounts, why the over-75s don't pay for their TV licences,
> why we still have the ridiculous winter fuel allowance, and
> so on. Yet so successful were the baby boomers (no doubt
> because they're so very special, and also good at hip things
> like the saxophone) that these indicators no longer apply.

The saxophone crack seems a bit desperate. But focus, for a moment, on the word 'ridiculous', and juxtapose it with the report issued, and widely publicised, on 13 February 2012 (a wretchedly cold month, my diary glumly records). The following is from the *Telegraph*, under the grim headline 'Hypothermia deaths double over five years'. I'll quote at length:

> Figures revealed that 1,876 patients were treated in hospital
> for the condition in 2010/11, an increase from 950 in 2006/07.

The number who died within 30 days of being admitted rose from 135 to 260.

Three quarters of those admitted to hospital with hypothermia were over-60s, with cases rising among that age group more than any other – from 633 to 1,396.

The statistics, released by the NHS Information Centre, cover a period in which soaring energy bills have been pushing more and more pensioners into fuel poverty – meaning they are forced to choose between heating and eating.

An industry analyst, uSwitch has calculated that in 80% of home[s] energy is being rationed, and called for a cut in VAT on energy bills.

Campaigners on behalf of the elderly said it was scandalous that in modern-day Britain, pensioners could be dying from hypothermia.

The figures come as Britain has been suffering from a prolonged cold snap with temperatures plunging as low as minus 18.3C (minus 0.94F) last week.

Hypothermia takes place when body temperature falls below 35C (95F) from its usual 37C (98.6F), with symptoms including violent shivering, confusion, delirium and unconsciousness.

The new figures show that while the rise in admissions of those suffering from the illness has been greatest among the over-60s, there have been increases among all age groups, the *Daily Mail* reported.

Cases have risen by 54% to 276 among those aged 15 to 59, while there were 50 hypothermia cases among children aged 14 and under in 2010/11, a 22% increase.

The statistics on deaths are not broken down by age.

Meanwhile over the same period the price of gas has gone up by 40% while electricity now costs 21% more.

Age UK says the number of older people living in fuel poverty has tripled since 2003, now representing three million people, or a quarter of all pensioners.

While the elderly receive cold weather payments if the temperature falls below a certain level … campaigners argue that the money is not enough to stop people contracting hypothermia in many cases.

A survey by Age UK last month found half of pensioners had turned their heating down to save money even when they were not warm enough, with many so cold that they go to bed before they are tired or stay in one room, to keep bills down.

Charity director Michelle Mitchell said: 'We like to think of ourselves as a civilised society which protects the most vulnerable. The fact that there are still older people who are suffering and dying of hypothermia is deeply shocking.'

The hypothermia figures come as the parent companies of Britain's six big energy firms are expected to announce total profits of £15 billion in the next few weeks.

I personally don't find the above figures at all 'ridiculous'. We are not talking chilblains but actual deaths. Is it 'ridiculous' to try to do something, however tokenistic, to prevent people from dying in pain? Yes, apparently, if they are old people. Is Rifkind of the ancient Greek persuasion, a man who would leave babies on hillsides overnight for the assurance that they are up to the hurly-burly of life?

It was the findings of this Age UK report that led to the introduction of the winter fuel payment scheme, in November 2014. Some 500 OAPs having, one calculates, died of hypothermia in the interval. The mills of government grind slowly and it is easy to get crushed between their slow turn. Under the scheme, eligible old people of fixed address received between £100 and £300 tax-free to help pay for heating bills.

Hugo Rifkind opens his jolly assault with a frontal attack on 'baby boomers'. There is one BB whom he knows well. His father, the eminent Sir Malcolm Rifkind, was born in June 1946.

Rifkind Sr is a wholly admirable politician who has over many years devoted his formidable talents and energies to the welfare of his two countries – Scotland and England. But, smart as he is, he fell into an elephant trap in February 2015.

Having retired from Cabinet rank, and presumably unwilling to go to the living graveyard of 'the other place', he was invited, in a sting operation mounted by a couple of canny *Telegraph* reporters, to offer his services as a consultant. He might give his assistance as a private consultant for international business, it was suggested. As the newspaper reported: 'Sir Malcolm told [these] undercover reporters that he was "self-employed" despite receiving an MP's salary of £67,000 and said that he could arrange "useful access" to ambassadors because of his status.'

He further confided that his normal charge for his services was between £5,000 and £8,000 for half a day. My whole annual old-age pension is that amount. £200, my fuel allowance, comes out at a few minutes of Malcolm Rifkind's working time.

It was, Rifkind said in a candid, damage limitation interview on the *Today* programme the following day, a 'silly' slip to have said he was self-employed while receiving £67k plus expenses from the taxpayer. But no one judged him all that harshly – why should they? Malcolm Rifkind had done the state excellent services which far outweighed any late-life 'silliness', as he called it. And everyone knew the exit from Parliament was a revolving door into the world where real money, magnitudes greater than £67k, was made.

There are not 12 million Rifkinds in the BBB generation. But the bulk of those un-Rifkindish millions, scraping by on their £7k per annum, might justifiably feel a certain resentment. Nor might they feel that paltry £200 Gordon Brown (age 65) had given them 'ridiculous'. It's not enough, but it's not ridiculous. £16k a day for advice (and some embassy door-opening) might well be thought 'ridiculous'. I harp on the R-word because its jovial callousness pains me. I feel the cold terribly.[24]

The Over-75 Free TV Licence

How many over-75s in the UK? Make a guess. My guess, as one of their number, is probably around 9 per cent of the total population. And growing.[25]

The BBC reported on 25 January 2016:

> People over 75 may be asked to give up [I like that phrase] their free TV licence or make a voluntary contribution to it, under plans being considered by the BBC.
>
> The corporation must absorb the loss of £650m worth

---

24 Ever since, I like to think, the awful winter of 1947 and its fuel cuts. Parts of me have never thawed out, I fancy.

25 Accurate information is probably buried in http://www.ageuk.org.uk/Documents/EN-GB/Factsheets/Later_Life_UK_factsheet.pdf?dtrk=true. I can't, however, turn it up.

of licences for over-75s from 2020 as part of a funding deal agreed with ministers last year.

A report on ways to appeal for voluntary contributions is due in 2016.

The BBC has refused to comment on suggestions that older celebrities might front a publicity campaign.

The Times reported that such a campaign could be run by personalities such as Sir Michael Parkinson and actress Dame Helen Mirren.

Both of whom, of course, are rich 'personalities' thanks to their outstanding talents. Good for them.

Other statistical analyses, of a complicating tendency, came up around the same period with the fact that two million over-75s lived alone. Sixty per cent of them were women – 'relics', as Victorians called them, of a passed-away family life. 'Why', as Samuel Johnson rejoined when asked why he gave money to beggars in the street, which they would only spend on tobacco and drink, 'should they be denied such sweeteners of their existence?' There are, alas, few sweeteners of existence for the lonely over-75s. TV may well be one.

✻　✻　✻

These 'little things' that fuel rage against the old are tokenistic: trivial beyond serious consideration. Manifestly, they grate among the younger and middle-aged population at large; otherwise they would not be so repetitively and prominently brought forward. But, given the vast non-trivial sums the British government deals in, the amounts these payments involve are paltry.

'The winter fuel allowance', it is reported, 'costs between £2bn and £3bn a year, typically (it depends on the weather), while TV licences for those aged over 75 cost around £550 million. Once you add free bus passes and the like, the total cost comes to around £5 billion.'[26]

The pension 'triple lock' (it sounds like a nifty move in tae kwon do) is similarly trivial financially. But it, too, drives younger, non-receiving generations to volcanic spasms of irrational fury.

The history of the measure is, nonetheless, instructive. In 2000, Gordon Brown incurred what every politician

---

26　*Daily Telegraph*, 7 June 2012.

fears most, by raising the old-age pension by 75p a week. There were screaming front-page headlines in widely read newspapers and snide comments at PMQs.

No PM would make Brown's mistake again. In 2010, the grand-sounding 'triple lock' was introduced, specifically to keep the grey vote happy and shut up critics as to the government's manifest unfeelingness to the old.

By the terms of the triple lock, OAP payment was guaranteed to rise annually in line with whichever was the higher percentage: inflation, average earnings or 2.5 per cent. By 2016, the 'lock' had become, Ros Altmann complained, merely symbolic – and potentially risky. Altmann spoke with unusual authority on this matter. She was promoted baroness on the strength of her tenure as pension minister recently departed, after what was universally regarded as worthwhile service for the aged.

In early August, Altmann lobbied the government, via mass media releases, to kill the triple lock. It could prove to be 'enormously' expensive, she argued. And the savings from abolishing it should be 'hypothecated' for 'better causes'. The triple lock, she said, 'is a political construct, a totemic policy that is easy for politicians to trumpet, but from a pure policy perspective, keeping it for ever doesn't make sense'. What really drove Altmann to her protest, however, was the wholly realistic expectation that the government will keep the triple lock as distracting window dressing while furtively raising the qualification age for old-age benefits ('work till you drop, old Brits'). That remedy works wonderfully, for example, with members of the House of Lords, most of whom look like their own stuffed mummies, coming back to life only to collect their £300 per diem attendance allowance. It works less well for the average HGV driver, one might think, whose back is buggered by the age of 50 and who is forced to eke out twenty years on the meagre doles of 'sickness benefit'. A trifle less than £300 per diem, alas.

The old-age pension is, after the NHS, the biggest annual drain for the government. Around £9 billion is the current annual damage. And it's growing, year on year – less as a result of the triple lock than of demography.

But – at the receiving end – the triple lock is demonstrably pointless. It's a distraction from real financial pressures. A 2.5 per cent increase on the pension I got in 2015, on £119.30 pcm, yielded £3. Per month, that is. Not enough for a flat white and a copy of the morning paper at my local Costa.

What is required, to yield a decent old-age pension, is something analogous to the American social security charge on income, relative to the size of that income, with a flat universal benefit when the pension is eventually claimed (usually in the beneficiary's early sixties).[27] As it now stands in the US, assuming you have paid in for any ten years of your life, you will receive, until death, an amount considerably larger than the British OAP (as we no longer call it), and – with care – sufficient to scrape by on.

No British government recently, or in the foreseeable future, is willing to do what America has done. Hence our triple-lock absurdity.

---

27 The social security measure was brought in by Franklin Delano Roosevelt to ensure that the miseries of the Great Depression never again oppressed the American people. Its key feature is that the universal tax is correlated with income. But the pay-off, in late life, is 'flat'. And considerably more of a living wage than the British OAP.

Fight Back

'Whoosh!'
'What's that noise?'
'That's your life.'
'Can I have it back?'
'No.'

– OLD JOKE

Time is on their side – the old can't, in the long term, win because, quite simply, they're old. Their young foe will still be standing on the battlefield while the oldsters have gone to their reward underneath it.

Nonetheless, one can fight back and, in a state of comfortable siege, keep the young fuckers at bay for a good while. The Israelites, one recalls, did not win at Masada. But they made their point by holding out from the Romans for two years – better go down fighting, they resolved, than troop, like sheep, to the slaughterhouse. And, of course, when the battle was clearly lost, they killed themselves. The 'Roman death', as it was called. That was the one thing the Jews would take from their oppressors.

Before detailed advice, some brief, summary instruction for the age warrior. Buy two books: (1) Karol Sikora's *The Street-Wise Patient's Guide to Surviving Cancer* (the advice – on how to 'game' the NHS – is transferable to all worrying medical conditions); (2) The third edition of Derek Humphry's assisted suicide manual, *Final Exit*, if your thoughts go Roman/Israelite. It's helpful, additionally, to assemble a 'suicide pack', and find a local hardware store which sells pure-grade helium across the counter.

Buy, in addition, a copy of David Willetts's *The Pinch: How the baby boomers took their children's future – and why they should give it back* and use it for toilet paper. Guilt weakens; avoid it.

I am not a qualified doctor, counsellor, therapist, financial adviser, lawyer, priest or trainer. I am not qualified for anything except writing and talking about English Literature, which is scarcely the point here. Or in most places, alas. What follow are 'tips' – things I have picked up, or identified as helpful, from personal experience, observation and reading in the fight against what is being done to those of my time of life. Fight is, I believe, the appropriate word.

The tips may not be universally helpful or appropriate. Every personal situation, at this late juncture of life, is different. Do not, for that very reason, accept the homogenisations ('seniors', 'aged', 'elderly'). They mean nothing and are often no more than packaging, the better to dispose of you.

Our days have been prolonged: prolonged in many cases to a time when we will no longer fear death because with the insentience of dementia we will know neither that we are old nor that we are dying.

– WILLIAM MILLER, IN *LOSING IT* – ANOTHER BOOK TO BUY AND PONDER

I stress the point made above: regard the following as going beyond mere survival into active self-assertion in the face of what is inevitable and, although it cannot be reversed, can be confronted and contested. And fought.

97

Stay Fit

Deterioration of the brain (or, at least, its shrinking after the age of 60) seems to be something you have to expect, assuming you are lucky enough to live long enough. You can never, once you are down that path, re-emerge into your former clear-mindedness. In as many as one in three of those who live to the longevity limit, mental cloudiness will become acute. Your cerebral cortex will follow your biceps.[28] I would like to think that both can, to some extent, be preserved in good shape.

Those spared the worst mental decay will probably still experience some degree of malfunction – if only a slowing of reflexes and the imperative of, for example, giving up your driving licence and mountain climbing. No more north face of the Eiger. Medical science has no immediate expectation of a cure – or even any effective means of surgically or pharmaceutically arresting the progress of Alzheimer's, vascular dementia or

---

28 The decay of bodily musculature is dramatic after 60 – although it can be mitigated by regular workouts. It's always been a mystery to me that a supposedly well-meaning local government doesn't give the elderly free gym passes as well as, or instead of, bus passes.

those other afflictions which used to be called 'softening of the brain'. Arteries harden, brains soften. The way of all flesh.

Doctors' best advice is: 'What's good for the heart is good for the head.' What, precisely, does this mean? It is simple. Eat right. Cut down on red meat; bump up vegetables and fruit; avoid salt; don't, above all, smoke; stay around 120/70 blood pressure and less than 70 pulse rate. Keep your weight within the recommended BMI and low thirties waist size.

You will never know precisely where the enemy will strike. But what carried your parents and grandparents to their reward is often useful predictively. Sometimes preventively. Adopt a strategy of all-round defence. Lengthen the odds where you are able. Join a gym that emphasises body strength, not athletic fitness. Exercise in gyms, or on dance floors, which have a preponderance of members younger than you are. Never clique with people your own age.

Tolerance for drink collapses catastrophically with age, and it's humiliating to wet your bed on what used hardly to wet your whistle. Not to mention oesophageal cancer, cirrhosis, broken marriage and those other late-drinking-career afflictions.

If you desperately need some recreational substance, use either marijuana or ecstasy – both of which the older frame can handle reasonably well, and which are highly pleasurable. And if you're stopped by the police, chances are they will never in a hundred years think you're carrying. If, as I do, you spend a lot of time in southern California, you'll notice the clientele of the medical marijuana clinics includes many seniors. In the UK, supply, and quality stuff, is best done through a young person you trust. Hanging around dodgy street corners is very risky.

Myself, I over-indulge in coffee. There are four of us in my marriage (to echo Princess Di): me, my wife, my Nespresso machine and my dog.

Fitness Further Considered

Get a dog to walk you (not you it) if you can't face the local sweat factory and the intimacies of the gym locker room. It's not really 'exercise' but it is therapeutically de-stressing. And dogs love you unconditionally. You can't say that about the Nespresso machine and sometimes even your spouse.

For those faster on their pins, there was a slightly perplexing, but fascinating, news story in mid-February 2012, linking walking speed with the onset of dementia. As reported in *Psych Central*, it's thought-provoking enough to quote at length:

> Determining a middle-age individual's risk for dementia may be as simple as timing walking speed and assessing hand grip strength.
>
> New research presented at the American Academy of Neurology's Annual Meeting showed that these tests can be predictive.
>
> 'These are basic office tests which can provide insight into risk of dementia and stroke and can be easily performed by a neurologist or general practitioner,' said Erica C. Camargo, MD, MSc, PhD, with Boston Medical Center.

In the study, more than 2,400 men and women with an average age of 62 underwent tests for walking speed, hand grip strength and cognitive function. At the same time, brain imaging studies were also performed.

During the follow-up period of up to 11 years, 34 people developed dementia and 70 people had a stroke.

The study found people with a slower walking speed in middle age were one-and-a-half times more likely to develop dementia compared to people with faster walking speed.

Strength appears predictive among older individuals as stronger hand grip strength was associated with a 42 percent lower risk of stroke or transient ischemic attack (TIA) in people over age 65.

This was not the case, however, for people in the study under age 65.

'While frailty and lower physical performance in elderly people have been associated with an increased risk of dementia, we weren't sure until now how it impacted people of middle age,' said Camargo.

Investigators discovered that slower walking speed is linked to lower total cerebral brain volume and poorer performance on memory, language and decision-making tests.

Furthermore, stronger hand grip strength was correlated with larger total cerebral brain volume as well as better performance on cognitive tests asking people to identify similarities among objects.

Investigators say that additional research is necessary to determine how and why the relationships exist.

'Further research is needed to understand why this is happening and whether preclinical disease could cause slow walking and decreased strength,' said Camargo.

One notes, with some gratification, that for these American researchers, 65 years counts as 'middle-aged'. And perhaps, if you are going to buy a dog, you should make it a greyhound.

My own hunch is that the walking speed is less a pre-condition than evidence that the examinee has, over many years, kept themselves in good shape and, in consequence, kept the hated things of late age at bay. At the very least, exercise, briskly done, releases endorphins, nature's antidepressants.

Stay Active

For the older person, being bustlingly active is probably more the issue than supreme, muscle-flexing and speed hiking, physical fitness – although the two merge into each other. Get a Fitband – it measures activity ('steps') of all kinds usefully. Even bustling in the kitchen or garden.

Activity has another aspect to it. What might be called taking charge of your own life. The old are (when not mad as hell) more prone than other age groups to deference in the presence of authority. Medical practitioners become more authoritative figures – godlike, even – in one's universe as one ages. It's common for older patients to take their medicine lying down (physically and metaphorically) and too usual for doctors, under increasing work pressure, to prescribe a pill rather than invest time in a more thoughtful, time-consuming consultation. Who can blame them?

The advice is to insist. Actively. But do so politely (Karol Sikora's advice). Insist, most importantly, on prophylactic and diagnostic screening (wellness checks) for such things as PSA (one of the tests for prostate

PART III

cancer – not entirely reliable, but helpful – see below)
and the best kinds of treatment. Unspoken as it is, there
is a climatic sense among the caring and curing professions that 'you've had a good run, time to let things
take their course'.

I note, for example, that the latest invitation for a general check-up from my GP (dated 3 February 2012) tells
me: 'We are inviting you to attend a free NHS Health
Check. NHS Health Checks are being offered to people
aged between 40 and 74 once every five years.'

This meant, aged 73, I was entering my last-chance-
saloon years. After 74, it's 'good luck and die in your
own time, not ours', apparently. The medical check itself
looks somewhat basic. I speak after twenty-five years of
annual checks, under Blue Shield, in the US, in which
even toenail fungus, dandruff or suspicious moles invisible to the naked eye are prospected for potential threats.

What the NHS offers, as I understand it, is a blood
pressure test, a pinprick blood cholesterol test, and the
usual stuff with the stethoscope on heart and lungs,
plus some background enquiries as to family and personal health history. As it happens, I check my blood

pressure every day at home, buy statins over the counter, and have worked out, for myself, the way my genetic dice are loaded.

I advise going to young dentists and opticians (their apparatus gets better every year, and the youthful practitioners know it best) and old doctors, specifically the one who has known you best over the years. I also spend a lot of time with Dr Google. Family doctors, who know whole generations over decades, are a thing of the past. No more Kildare or Doctor Finlay's Casebook (you will have to be over 60 to have the faintest idea what those allusions mean).

Drugs

The BBB generation hitting 65 in the second decade of the twenty-first century is the most knowledgeable ever, and hippest, where 'substances' are concerned. Little helpers come in two forms: prescription and street. There was, in February 2012, an exhibition devoted to the 'pill' in London's Wellcome Gallery (a research institution spun off from the hugely successful pharmaceutical firm). Ian Jack visited it, and wrote a smart piece about it in *The Guardian* (18 February):

> A bulky paper bag with a prescription form attached awaits us. The pills have begun. To women, a regime of pills may be no big deal in a life that may have been governed since the age of 16 by the contraceptive pill; and women, to risk a generalisation, are less alarmist about medicine. But to many men, pills are a sign of vulnerability – sometimes the first sign. Cholesterol, hypertension, type-two diabetes: our 50-year-old selves were hardly aware of the prospect of them. And now 10 and more years later they come marching towards us with their little warning banners about heart attacks, a risk to be moderated by an unending commitment to pills.

A man of 80, the exhibition declares, will pop more pills in the last ten years of his life than in the previous seventy. He'll rattle his way to the grave.

I pop quite a few little helpers. My observations are as follows. Cialis, 5mg daily, is necessary, to counteract penile atrophy, after the kind of surgical history I've had (prostatectomy; let's not get into details). It has other effects which may or may not be welcome and no other unwelcome side effects that I observe. It is expensive (£90 pcm). The NHS, if pestered, will give me four Viagra tablets a month. They have a rather strict notion on the frequency of sexual intercourse.

I have, at periods, been on Lisinopril for blood pressure, and hate it for the dry night cough it causes. But it works. Buy an upper-arm cuff blood pressure monitor (two machines is best – to make sure the readings match). I take baby aspirin tablets, daily. Cost, if generic, minimal. There are very good corticosteroid allergy remedies (I currently use Pirinase – £10 for a month's supply). I used to be tormented with hay fever – particularly in the year-round pollination of southern California, and hot-damp English summers. For years I couldn't find relief with antihistamines because of the drastic effect on my then inflamed prostate, before it went the way of my tonsils, appendix and wisdom teeth in younger life.

Close friends tell me confidentially that antidepressants (Seroquel, for example) are effective but have heavy side effects (on body weight, excretion etc.). For those in extreme pain, oramorph (orally taken morphine) is efficacious, I observe, from hospital visiting mainly. So is Vicodin, Prozac and Oxycontin, but dangerous for those, like myself, predisposed to addiction. I've been offered them – off prescription, as a pick-me-up – but invariably turn them down. Their nickname, 'hillbilly heroin', is a warning.

I have never smoked tobacco (although I've ingested plenty of second-hand smoke) and haven't touched alcohol for thirty years – I like it too much to trust myself. I have little to say about harder drugs other than what is above. I occasionally go to AA/NA meetings and hear horrific things about 'speed' and 'K' and 'coke'. My feeling for those in later life is to avoid everything which isn't certifiably healthful and not dangerous.

'Lifestyle changes' should be the first choice; what one could call the probiotic yoghurt trail. Homeopathic remedies, my distinguished pharmacological friend David Colquhoun (http://dcscience.net/) tells me, are, where not actually poisonous, generally useless. 'Simples to cure cancers', Philip Larkin calls them in

'Church Going'. Neither professor nor poet thinks well of them. I take their word and keep my money. Vitamin pills, ditto. They simply enrich Big Pharma and quacks.

Retirement

It is most wisely regarded as a change of occupation rather than withdrawal from the workplace. It is, as I have observed, very hard to work yourself to death, but relatively easy to retire yourself to death. It depends on too many factors to generalise. But do something, gainful or voluntary, to fill the empty hours. The truly abysmal quality of daytime TV helps. Need you, however, retire at all in this day and (at your) age? Do not, unless you are saintly by nature, go gently (as Dylan Thomas's poem sensibly instructs) into the night. Recent legislation (introduced from Brussels in 2005) has gone a long way to abolishing the mandatory retirement age in the UK. Use it. It's an interesting speculation that, post-Brexit, the UK may abolish the reform and go back to mandatory retirement, to make way for angry youth at the entry point into the most desirable professions. We shall see.

In the US, age-enforced retirement has been illegal for two decades. It doesn't, in my experience (which is not universal, but revealing) mean that you are, like Ben-Hur, chained to your oar until merciful release in the shape of the undertaker. What, in my experience (working in the US), it means is that you expect a golden parachute. As one of my grumpier colleagues (an eminent astronomer, occupant of a professorial chair) put it to me: 'I'm going to sit on the fucking thing till they buy me out of it.' Which they duly did. Hal walked a golden path to his retirement years.

The EU legislation abolishing the legality of the default retirement age can, in some professions, be used to haggle your way to a more comfortable departure. If you do fall on your sword, or are pushed, don't believe the warm words and statements of continuing connection that come with the gold watch. Once you're out of the door, you're yesterday. Former colleagues will be unfailingly kind and courteous when you meet them, but somehow they're never available for the lunch they vaguely promise you must have.

In their hearts – though they will be too polite to

say so – they see themselves as players and you are out of the game. But are you? Not always. Two things you acquire over the years are (typically) skill and contacts. It's surprising how much freelance work is there to be picked up. Since you no longer have a career – but are merely looking for jobs – you don't have to be proud. Lower your standards, if necessary.

In February 2012, the veteran stand-up comedian Jackie Mason (1931–2030), an ex-rabbi, announced that his forthcoming visit to London would be his last. Asked on Newsnight *by its arts correspondent, Stephen Smith, if this meant no more public performances, Mason replied: 'No, give me a hundred thousand dollars and I'll tell you a joke.'*

Cryogenics: Live and Fight Another Day

Non omnis moriar, says the Latin poet: not all of me will die. Cerebral cryo-preservation is expensive but, if you are into life extension, it's probably no worse than the

14 million to 1 chance of winning the lottery. Depositing your brain in the brain bank is one thing; withdrawing it in functioning order is, however, something else. Reanimation from cryonic suspension doesn't yet work. Expanding the shrunken tissue to its mid-life healthiness ditto. But a surprising number of older people (Americans mainly, so far) are willing to take a gamble on the ingenuity of science. Walt Disney allegedly did. He probably didn't, but I like the myth. He was, after all, the creator of the sleeping princess in the film that entranced me as a child.

Going rates for neurosuspension in the US are: whole body $130k (Walt's putative choice), whole head $50k, whole brain a snip at $25k. Any number of American brain banks offer their chilly services to potential organ savers. You can get details from the market leader, Alcor (www.alcor.org). My personal feeling is that it's strictly something for rich fools. But if you can't be foolish when old, when can you?

A good novel has been written on this theme – *Zero K* (2016) by Don DeLillo (aged 79). Well worth a skim.

Teach Yourself Finance

This is more sensible than freezing your neurons. Among my acquaintance, few seem to have benefited from the advice of 'financial advisers', a genus which seems as attracted to the old people as barnacles to the bottoms of old boats. But more predatory than that harmless crustacean. Many friends of mine have become seriously poor from financial advice they paid for. The word 'piranha' has been mentioned. As early as possible, learn all you can about keeping your assets, and wealth, safe. Converting it to gold and putting it under the floorboards like Silas Marner (see above) is, usually, more sensible than the smooth patter from the young man in the suit who lives on the commissions he can extract from suckers like you (and me).

But then, of course, there may come a time when you can't physically lift the floorboards or mentally remember which floorboard it is you put your gold under. Or someone else may notice where you put it and help themselves before the reading of the will (Silas Marner, you'll recall, comes to grief that way).

A lawyer friend, just a little younger than yourself,

is ideal – not least because lawyers, unlike financial advisers, fear professional sanctions for wrongdoing. But, in the spare time made available by retirement, bone up yourself on benefits, retirements and all that brain-stretching stuff about ISAs. Or attend seminars on the subjects that aren't trying to sell you anything but information. There are attractive postgraduate MBA courses for those who are really keen. I've known acquaintances who've grown rich on draw-downs from their pensions. I personally don't have the brain for it.

Sheltered Accommodation

If you need it, you need it. But you get what you pay for; not a scruple more or less. Make escape plans before you enrol. And, if possible, a trial stay – as a paying guest, not a committed resident. There's a certain feel of 'abandon hope all ye who enter here', I observe. Diana Athill (98 years), in her late-life ruminations (see, e.g., *Alive, Alive Oh!: And Other Things That Matter*, 2015 – yet another book for your oldster library), is very sound on how to choose the best last 'home' and make the best of it. She's very amusing about using her motorised wheelchair with the ruthlessness of a Panzer rampaging over the Russian steppes in 1941.

Organise

Britain sadly lacks something equivalent to the AARP (the American Association of Retired Persons). The AARP lobbies politicians, who listen attentively because the old voters actually vote. Senior Americans not only cast their vote, they do so on single issues that are important to senior Americans – things like prescription charges, Medicare (including medical marijuana; were they not children of the 1960s?), euthanasia and, most of all, social security. American politicians fear the grey electorate. They have good reason to. If there is one thing which, in my view, would help the old in their fight, it is the creation of a cis-Atlantic BARP (the acronym has a nice ring to it, I think; rather like what one does after a slap-up meal).

There are 35 million paid-up members of AARP, the cutting edge of the country's 70 million citizens over the age of 50. AARP votes swing elections. For climatic reasons, retirees cluster in swing states like Florida, or where the cost of living is low, as in the mid-west, another 2016 battleground. The older voters are numerous where it most counts. And, as I say, given their special interests, they tend to vote en bloc.

AARP was founded in 1958 by Dr Ethel Percy Andrus, a retired high-school principal. The estimable Andrus wanted one thing primarily: healthcare for seniors who were, because of their unfortunate habit of falling ill, uninsurable privately. AARP flexed its lobbying muscle and the result, five years later, was Medicare: free, top-quality healthcare for all Americans over 65. In the US, contrary to the UK, the older you are, the better care you get.

AARP nowadays has a paid staff of 1,800 and an annual operating budget of $600 million (£334 million). It aims, as its mission statement grandly declares, to make America 'a society in which everyone ages with dignity and purpose'. To that end, it agitates ferociously on the three issues American seniors most care about: the state pension, Medicare and prescription charges.

Because of AARP, American seniors get a better shake than their British counterparts. Do the maths. American social security (which you can collect at 62, if you have paid in for ten years) yields around $12,000 a year. The basic British pension of £113 a week, plus pennies, furnishes less than half the purchasing power.[29] Britain awaits its Dr Andrus. Upton Sinclair said it all at the end of his novel *The Jungle*: 'Organise, organise.'

Until British OAPs organise to set up a British Association of Retired Persons, they will suffer the fate of all old animals in the jungle.

How to Spend It

David Hume called money 'abstract happiness'. You should consider removing it from the realm of the abstract into the concrete. Realise your financial assets. In both senses. The old, because they are old and because of the wonders of compound interest, will often find themselves surprisingly well off. And, consequently,

---

29 Post-Brexit, with the collapse of sterling, the relative values are even lower.

powerful. If there is a novel to read on this topic, it's H. G. Wells's *The Sleeper Awakes*. A man goes into a coma and wakes a century later. He is, he discovers, the richest man in the world thanks to the appreciation of his (initially modest) bank balance. A lot of old people are in an analogous situation. If the years have been good to you financially, the problem is what to do with their assets? Piddle it out, selflessly, on the young in what John Major used to call the 'golden cascade'?[30] Or lavish it, selfishly, on number one? (See, above, the bumper sticker 'I'm spending my children's patrimony'.) Give it to the Battersea Dogs Home? Personally I recommend selfish. The number one option.

Socialise

The family, as a unit, is much disintegrated in modern times. Very often, however, whether single or partnered, you find yourself in a family house with no family. One very good idea, successfully done by one of my friends,

---

30 What London telephone boxes, with their saucy postcards, did Sir John get that image from, one wonders. Saucily.

is to recruit a university student (preferably female, with good domestic training in her family background) to live in – on commuted rent, in return for cleaning one day and stocking the fridge/pantry two days a week. The huge new fees exacted from undergraduates (particularly overseas students) give you a strong hand to fill the socket where family used to be. With the added bonus of aiding higher education.

Maintain

Much of one's daily time is taken up with maintenance, at all stages of life. The maths are familiar: eight hours for sleep, three hours for food, two hours just moving from here to there, two hours shopping, eight hours earning the money to spend shopping. 'Living' is squeezed into ever shorter packets, hurried, or put off till the weekend or the vacation. Or, of course, retirement.

One of the things you have to reckon, as you age, is that, as with old cars, maintenance is ever more time-consuming (doctor's waiting rooms etc.) and costlier. You walk into your dentist and you are £500

pounds poorer. But it's important: build more time into
your schedule, though.

Observe

In one of his poems, Philip Larkin describes mothers at
a children's playground as being pushed to the side of
their own lives. The same description applies to age. It
goes along with a feeling of uselessness, but also gives
one the privilege of seeing things more clearly – as, from
his position in the wings of life's stage, does Larkin. If
you still have a brain that works as well as ever, thinking
about life is one of the interesting pleasures of late-life.
Read (alone, or in a group). Philosophise. Or, if you're
Larkin-inclined, poeticise.

Do all these things and, with luck, you'll emerge from
this war in good fighting shape. For as long as you're
lucky enough to last.

A Personal Afterword

A T THIS TERMINAL point, I'll allow myself to divagate into memoir. Talking about myself if only to myself. I am old, in the Father William stage of life. People, aiming to flatter me, say, 'You only look 65', i.e. 'old', but not 'very old'.

Aspects of my case illustrate some nooks and crannies which may, I hope, supplement the main sections of the foregoing polemic. And, at the end of it all, everything is personal. And solitary. 'We live as we dream: alone,' said Joseph Conrad. It's a truth which comes home when the living and dreaming one's enjoyed in life is nearly done.

Prostateless, I Take My Leave

If pneumonia once had the sobriquet 'old man's friend',

prostate cancer ('PC') is the 'old man's enemy'. It is the second most common cancer killer of elderly males. Its red zone starts around 50.

There are 50,000 cases a year in the UK, the majority in men aged 65+. One in eight men will be diagnosed with the disease in their late-lifetime. There are some 11,000 UK deaths a year from PC – enough for it to qualify as an epidemic. The novelist Philip Roth (age 83), whose serial hero, Nathan Zuckerman, lives with a botched prostate operation, rendering him impotent, incontinent and philosophical, has called prostate cancer the worst 'plague' afflicting his elderly generation. For guys only, of course.

PC is, as it happens, eminently curable – but there are complications in deciding how to bring that happy result about. There may well be pockets of the familiar NHS negligence + indifference attitude, where the old are concerned, in treating PC – but there are better practical reasons for NHS triage, and disinclination to act promptly, where this nasty disease is concerned. In the US, it is reckoned, 'One man in six will be diagnosed with prostate cancer during his lifetime, but only one man in thirty-five will die from it.' Most will survive because their PC will never reach full lethality. Or some other more lethal thing pops in first.

The prostate gland clenches round the bladder and urethra. Why God invented the damn thing is not clear. At least not to me. But it somehow facilitates ejaculation and, thereby, the continuation of the human race. The little bugger grows in a man's later years, after its primary biological function has usually passed. Peanut, walnut, coconut. It's unstoppable. If only one's penis grew likewise.

When enlarged, the prostate commonly causes urinary urgency. Most painfully, nocturnal enuresis – the desperate need to get up in the night. Suddenly the old-fashioned chamber pot (the 'gesunder') seems worth having, particularly if your bathroom is stairs away. At a crisis point, this condition, BPH (benign prostatic hyperplasia) can cause AUR (acute urinary retention). Many old men get to know what these acronyms mean and what the physical conditions they categorise feel like. Shit.

AUR is total blockage. The bladder, denied relief,

swells to breaking point like an overfull dam. In this situation 'benign' is something of a misnomer: backed up urine can do damage, lethal damage in extreme cases, to the kidneys. Wait too long and you're on dialysis for whatever life remains to you.

BPH is non-cancerous. PC is more dangerous and, dangerously, asymptomatic until it's advanced – and then much less treatable. In the 1970s, a simple blood test for what is called PSA (prostate-specific antigen) was devised specifically to diagnose prostate cancer. A doctor (God bless him) called T. Ming Chu invented it at the Roswell Park Cancer Institute. As the institute proudly proclaims on its website: 'About 25 years ago, the diagnosis of prostate cancer was the equivalent of a death sentence. Back then, only 4% of prostate cancers we diagnosed were curable. Now, with PSA, the cure rate is between 80% and 90%.'

Effectively, Dr Chu's test measures what the prostate is discharging into the bodily system. If performed early, it does so before the cancer is dangerous and when it is eminently curable.

In a healthy young man, the PSA count is in the low

single digits, year in year out. It rises with age and, with abnormalities (cancer among them), indicates something is going wrong.

PSA is a primary warning of PC. But the sneaky thing is: (1) PSA is not always accurate or standard across the older generation of males. It's volatile. Even too vigorous a cycle ride to the clinic can inflame it; (2) PC itself does not always kill. It can be 'sleepy' or 'tigerish'; there's no way, at the moment, of knowing which it is; (3) sufferers of PC are, often, so old that – as the tediously repeated saying iterates – old men die *with* PC, not *of* PC. There are delays, the cancer breaks out, metastasises, and the outlook is much bleaker.

There are other tests. A DRE (Digital Rectal Exam – effectively, being sympathetically sodomised by a knowing index finger) will feel for tell-tale bumps and corrugations. That's usually the first investigative procedure. After the PSA, and possibly the investigative finger, have raised suspicions, the next diagnostic step is a biopsy (like being shot up the anus by something halfway between an airgun and a banana). This procedure will recover needle samples from around the gland.

These dozen or so samples will turn up any cancerous tissue in the small area they have pricked. The biopsy is unpleasant while it's happening and afterwards. And damned humiliating. There is, apparently, some progress to moving beyond the current medieval inspections via blood test. Too late for me, alas.

With a positive result, treatment becomes a tricky thing. If you tell a man, in his vigorous sixties and seventies, for instance, that he has a growing cancer inside him, in an area he regards as vital to his personal sense of 'manhood', what should the oncologist recommend?

In the UK, the preferred response tends to be 'watch and wait'. It means every few months more PSA blood tests, more invasive fingers, and, yet again, the loaded rectal banana up your rear end.

Or, there are operative treatments. Some use accurately directed HIFU (high-intensity focused ultrasound), some use the old-fashioned surgical knife (open prostatectomy), some the delightfully named Da Vinci 'robotic' prostatectomy, with the surgeon in the other room (what apparently Andrew Lloyd Webber, and I suspect John Kerry, chose in America, where it's more readily available). Rudy Giuliani went for radium seeds, an exotic option. Bafflingly, these alternative solutions, along with watch and wait, are laid before the old man with PC, on a 'take your pick' principle.

Many will reflexively choose prostatectomy: cut the damn thing out and let me get on with my life, or what's left of it. The manly option. But the operation is frowned upon in the UK, as I observe it. It's very expensive. It lasts hours in the operating theatre. A small slip, among bundled nerves, can have disastrous consequences – the surgeon requires expertise. And any general operation under general anaesthetic has its risks for anyone, not least the elderly man.

Then, ironically, post-operative biopsy may indicate the cancer was neither really advanced nor, by nature, aggressive. All that NHS money had been spent for nothing. You could have done twenty-five cataract operations with it.

The operation, even when successful, has unpleasant sequels. In most cases it will entail months, or a lifetime, of post-operative incontinence (pads by day, catheter by night).

'Emission' and 'ejaculate' will be things of the past – it's retrograde, the semen washes back into the body for waste disposal. Assuming, that is, you can achieve erection. Erectile dysfunction is common after a successful prostate operation. It rather puts a question mark over 'successful' for many men.

Daily Viagra is recommended (the NHS allows four tablets a month). And, to cap it all, the operation takes a chunk off your 'endowment', as it's coyly called.

I'm in that condition of life where I have more dead friends than living friends. Quite some number of them have died (unnecessarily, in my view) of PC. What happens, after PC has broken out of the prostatic capsule, is that you get a persistent bone-ache in a particular bone – your back, or your ribs, say.

Persistent aches are par for the course after the age of 60. But these get worse. What happens then is palliative or standard cancer treatments designed to arrest further spread. Your body is now a free-fire zone for this roaming predator.

Early warning and follow-up would forestall this dire

outcome. But the UK system does not routinely offer old men the PSA test, although your GP is obliged to give you one should you demand it. Most old men don't know PSA from BBC.

If the PSA is at all concerning, and if you are persistent, you may get yourself through all the hoops. But it's not easy. Nor, some would say, should it be. If those 11,000 men who die every year had the facts put before them, they would, quite likely, go for the cleansing knife. It would be hugely expensive and, quite possibly, it would be unnecessary in a large number of cases. And the old themselves might not want to go to the grave in nappies with a drooping John Thomas.

But, one can't help suspecting, there is an unstated feeling that old men aren't worth huge amounts of specialist time and cash for what will be a few years of late life. Unless, that is, they are very important or very rich – in which case all plugs are pulled out. See the above sections and, if you find yourself in this situation, or one analogous – such as late-life breast cancer – fight for what might be your last rights.

Mein Kampf

At this point I can become totally anecdotal.

In the 1990s and early years of the twenty-first century, I was working, with a split professorial appointment, two-thirds of the year in London, a third in the US. One of the killer statistics bandied about in the dog-fight over 'Obamacare', at that period, was that under the UK's 'socialised' medicine, 57 per cent of men with prostate cancer survive to die of something else. In the US, under 'free-world' medicine, that figure is 90 per cent. I believe those figures are true.

In the high-class American institution where I was working, I was covered by the best of 'plans', Blue Shield PP (personal physician), which incorporated an annual wellness test. It tested all the usual things: blood pressure, diabetes, HIV, lipids. But also for prostate cancer, via PSA.

Year in, year out, my PSA was an unworrying 3 on the scale. Then, out of the blue, it went up to 7 in 2007 and 10 in 2008 and kept rising. 'Velocity' – the speed of rise – is a lead indicator for prostate cancer. I was told, in the result from my annual wellness test, to see an oncologist: now. It was stressed.

Every September in the UK is 'Prostate Cancer Awareness Month'. The truth is that the only thing that makes a fellow really 'aware' is when he hears the ominous words: 'I'm sorry to tell you, John, the biopsy reveals that you have prostate cancer.' I had that message by phone, at 4.25 p.m. on 17 February 2009. I was 71 years old.

As Dr Johnson said, death sentences concentrate the mind wonderfully. But, of course, it's not a death sentence. Go to any of the websites for prostate cancer survivors[31] and the first thing you learn is that only one out of six who have this particular carcinoma die of it, even if it's left untreated. It's Russian roulette. With the barrel pointed at your testicles. 'Do you feel lucky, punk? Well, do you?' as the man said.

My situation forced me to engage, in a very practical way, with the current differences between the NHS and American healthcare. In California, I had top-notch health coverage. Under enlightened US law, my employer was obliged to continue that coverage,

---

31 The best is YANA – acronymic for 'You Are Not Alone'.

for minimal co-payment, for eighteen months after my leaving their employ. No exclusions. I could, therefore, have state of the art treatment at somewhere such as Cedars-Sinai. It would cost me not a cent.

But I was also covered by the NHS. What would you choose with killer cells multiplying like homicidal lice in your groin? I decided on surgery. But which nation's healing scalpel? One thing that strikes you, after you've done some research, is that the best treatment for prostate cancer has always been pioneered in America.

Why has America led the way against this horrible scourge of elderly men? Follow the money. Males in the red zone for prostate cancer (roughly 50–80-year-olds) are the most lucratively insured sector of the US population. American medicine is not a 'service'; it's an 'industry', driven by the bottom line. The spin-off? Research and development goes where the dollars are. Old guys have the deep pockets.

Now cross the Atlantic. You're holding the NHS purse strings and have the following dilemma: (1) A one-month-old baby with a hole in the heart. Cost to cure: x pounds; (2) A 30-year-old woman with breast cancer. Cost to cure: x pounds; (3) A 70-year-old man with prostate cancer. Cost to cure: x pounds ... but you only have 2x pounds to hand out.

Whom do you throw overboard from the lifeboat? The iron law of triage in the UK tilts the board against the superannuated prostate sufferer. America throws the (often unremunerative) babies overboard, which is why, as Michael Moore crows in the film *Sicko*, it has higher infant mortality than Cuba. And old guys strike out.

So, being an elderly man, I should rationally have gone American: particularly as I had resolved, from the start, on robotic prostatectomy. But I didn't. Why not? The reason is everywhere on websites, where the consensus is: 'Go for the very best surgeon. And be sure to choose one who's done more than a thousand procedures.'

I could have tried for a leading Da Vinci specialist in Los Angeles. But so big is the robotic business in the US that those star surgeons have troops of young surgeons in training with them, all aiming to rack up their 1,000, making who knows how many errors on the way.

Well disposed as I am to teaching hospitals, I did not want to be some future starlet's apprentice work. I'm not that philanthropic.

If I wanted robotic surgery in the UK, the best person, a little research revealed, was Professor Roger Kirby. Kirby is forever raising charity money for prostate cancer treatment but – so expensive and in such short supply is the state of the art robotic machinery he uses – he charges. In point of fact, the charge is modest: less than the cost of every second car that passes you in the fast lane on the motorway. About half a four-door BMW, to be precise.

What should I do, I asked Kirby. I was not young. Ask yourself if you have ten good years ahead of you, he advised. I worked out that I did. Without cancer gnawing away at my innards, that was. There were some painful incisions on my wallet. But the histopathology revealed that the cancer had been expertly scooped out by Professor Kirby and his robot pal Leonardo. I felt lucky. And very grateful. But so many of my British friends, and people I knew of, were not lucky. They did not get treatment until too late. No ten years for them.

I went through the predicted dreary post-operative recovery process. If there is anything more lowering to the spirit than a quart-sized catheter half full of piss by your bed, I don't know it. But that was all seven years ago. All my PSA tests have, since the operation, revealed undetectable results. I may, indeed, get my ten good years. And after? Who knows. But they have been very good years for me, among the sweeter of my life. So far.

What then is my final advice to my male peers and their female partners? Fight for your right not to die.

Fight, that is, for your life, wherever you have to.

* * *

My theme throughout this short book has been that ageing is not merely a biological process. It involves a battle for survival and, at this particular juncture of history, is conveniently pictured as an intra-societal intergenerational civil war. In that conflict, wrongs are currently being perpetrated against the old. The evidence is all around us. I foresee little improvement in the near future.

I'll take my farewell on a pointy-headed professorial note. We know very little about the Anglo-Saxons and what we do know is enriched by the magnificent find of Sutton Hoo, in rural Suffolk. It was excavated in the year of my birth, just before World War Two.

A buried 'royal grave ship' was uncovered from the dirt, virtually intact as it had been buried in the sixth or seventh century. Who the royal figure, ruler of Suffolk's southern folk, was is unknown.

Death, the vessel made clear, was seen as not the end of life but a voyage from life. The richly artistic and valuable ornaments and artefacts the king was given to accompany him on his crossing bear witness to the high degree of culture and art achieved in those mis-named 'dark ages'.

One can make some fancifully contemporary observations. The royal personage (RP) was clearly a 'boat-blocker' – only one passenger. He was also, one may plausibly deduce, a 'house-hoarder'. He would for a certainty have owned, solely, his people's 'mead hall', where his retainers and soldiery wassailed by night. And, most spectacularly, he was a 'wealth-accumulator'.

Good for RP. One hopes he had a good trip – a kind of Viking River Cruise – into the hereafter. But what, if one looks at those relics in the British Museum, most strikes the eye? The weaponry he took with him. Finely crafted spears, wicked-looking daggers and a decorated sword. His emblem was the wolf (they roamed the woodlands of Suffolk in those far-off days; nowadays the citizen's main threat to life is the appalling A14 road, which the government has been promising to improve for years).

The moral a thoughtful person will draw from the Sutton Hoo treasures is clear. This person departed life as a warrior. He went to his end fighting the battle to live as fully, and as long, as a human being could. Follow his example.

My final advice is Dylan Thomas's beautiful, but terrifying, instruction to his aged dying father:

> Do not go gentle into that good night,
> Old age should burn and rave at close of day;
> Rage, rage against the dying of the light.

Rage on, old friends.

Postscript: Hot from the Keyboard

I am reading the proofs of this book on 31 October 2016, and take a break, eyes near bleeding point, for coffee and papers.

As usual, there was plentiful grist for my current mill. *The Times*, on this balmy last day of the month, winter coming in, had a number of relevant articles, none headline or screaming pieces: just page-fillers.

On page 2 there was: 'Triple-Lock Pension Too Generous, Says Duncan Smith'. It opens: 'The government is too generous to pensioners at the expense of the working poor and should abandon the triple lock [see above, pp. 91–4], Iain Duncan Smith said yesterday.'

With 'winding up' and resettlement costs, the average MP pension is £50k plus. The working poor are paying for that, as well.

On page 4 there is a story about NHS funding, expressing alarm at the pressure being put on the system by the 'ageing population'. The whole population ages a minute every minute. What the phrase means is 'the old'.

Below, on page 4, is another story headlined: 'Drug Rationing Will Devastate Lives, Charities Warn'. What particular 'lives' are at risk is revealed in the opening sentence: 'People with cancer and dementia will be denied treatment by "devastating" changes which put cost cutting before patients, charities have warned.'

For 'people' read 'old people': those most prone to cancer and dementia.

On page 8 the top story is 'Elderly Abuse Victims "Failed by Police and Prosecutors"'. It's another everyday article: one has read many like it before, many times. It opens:

> Hundreds of thousands of criminals are escaping punishment each year for preying on pensioners, with fewer than 1 per cent of cases ever reaching the courtroom, *The Times* can reveal.
>
> Only 0.7 per cent of all estimated crimes against people aged over 65 – ranging from neglect in care homes to burglaries and domestic abuse – result in criminal charges.

This is scandalous, but not news. And if one extrapolates the numbers, it is hundreds of thousands of crimes every year.

All this from one day's paper: most days' papers, one could argue. Who says it's not a war?